# My RV Travel Journal

Record your daily RV journey!

Attractions • Campground Info • Eats & Treats

Mileage Notes • Overnight Parking • Routes Followed • Routes to Avoid

Scenic Views • Weather Conditions • Wildlife Seen

And Much More!

Roundabout Publications

Published by:

Roundabout Publications
P.O. Box 569
LaCygne, KS 66040

Phone: 800-455-2207
Internet: www.RoundaboutPublications.com

ISBN-10: 1-885464-75-4
ISBN-13: 978-1-885464-75-0

| Date | Destination | Page |
|------|-------------|------|
|      |             |      |

| Date | Destination | Page |
|------|-------------|------|
|      |             |      |

# How to Use My RV Travel Journal

Below is an explanation of the different sections of the journal to be completed. This is helpful in understanding the various information you can include.

## Table of Contents

Fill in the blanks on the Table of Contents so you can easily find journal entries. There is space to enter the date, destination, and page number.

## The Journey

**Departure**: Enter the date and time of departure. You can also indicate if the day is a national holiday.

**Departed From**: Enter the name of the city, town, or other location you departed from on this date.

**Destination**: Enter the name of the city, town, or other location reached at the end of the day.

**Arrival**: Here you can make note of the time you arrived and the total number of hours driven on this day.

**Mileage**: Reference the mileage indicated on your odometer and enter the beginning, ending and total miles driven.

**Planned Travel Routes**: Here you can enter the roads and highways you plan to follow on today's journey.

## Along the Way

Make notes of the various things you encountered and experienced along the way. You may want to describe some of the attractions and points of interest seen. You may wish to write about some of the towns driven through or any stops made for lunch. Perhaps you enjoyed browsing through an antique store, a farmer's market, or other memorable shopping experience. Anything you'd like to remember about the day's journey can be written in this section.

## Day's End

**Stayed Overnight**: Make note of where you stayed for the night (in a campground or dry camping at Cracker Barrel, Walmart, or other location).

**Campground Name**: Enter the campground's name, your site number, and cost for the night.

**Campground Notes**: In this section, briefly describe the amenities available in the campground, indicate the noise level, and rate your overall experience.

**Overnight Parking Notes**: If you did not stay in a campground, you can describe where you parked for the night. You can also indicate the noise level and rate your overall experience.

**Dinner**: Use this to describe where you may have had dinner or whether you roasted hot dogs over a campfire!

**People Met Today**: Include the name of anyone you may have met this day. You can also make note of their phone number, mailing address or e-mail address.

## Miscellaneous Notes

Use this section to record miscellaneous notes about today's journey. Some suggestions are to note things you would like to see and do the next time you're in the area or the weather conditions experienced.

# The Journey

| Departure: | Date: | Time: | Holiday? ❑ Yes ❑ No |
|---|---|---|---|
| **Departed From**: | | | |
| **Destination**: | | | |
| **Arrival**: | Time: | Hours Traveled: | |
| **Mileage**: | Start: | End: | Total: |
| **Planned Travel Routes**: | | | |

# Along the Way

**My Notes Along the Way**:

*Suggestions:*

✧ *Attractions*

✧ *Cities and towns traveled through*

✧ *Eats and treats*

✧ *Points of interest*

✧ *Routes followed*

✧ *Routes to avoid*

✧ *Scenic views*

✧ *Shopping*

✧ *Wildlife seen*

✧ *Anything else you experience along the way!*

# Day's End

| Stayed Overnight: | ❑ Campground    ❑ Cracker Barrel    ❑ Walmart    ❑ Other: |
|---|---|
| **Campground Name:** | Site #:            Cost: |
| **Campground Notes:** | ❑ Full Hookups   ❑ 50-amp   ❑ Showers   ❑ Laundry   ❑ RV Dump   ❑ Wi-Fi   ❑ Camp Store |
| | *Noise:* ❑ Quiet ❑ Some ❑ Noisy ♦ *Overall:* ❑ Poor ❑ Fair ❑ Good ❑ Excellent |
| **Overnight Parking Notes:** | |
| | *Noise:* ❑ Quiet ❑ Some ❑ Noisy ♦ *Overall:* ❑ Poor ❑ Fair ❑ Good ❑ Excellent |
| **Dinner:** | |
| **People Met Today:** | |

# Miscellaneous Notes

| **Other Notes About Today's Journey:**  *Suggestions:*  ✧  *Things to see and do next time*  ✧  *Weather conditions*  ✧  *Anything else you want to remember!* | |
|---|---|

# The Journey

| Departure: | Date: | | Time: | Holiday?  ❑ Yes ❑ No |
|---|---|---|---|---|
| **Departed From**: | | | | |
| **Destination**: | | | | |
| **Arrival**: | Time: | | Hours Traveled: | |
| **Mileage**: | Start: | End: | | Total: |
| **Planned Travel Routes**: | | | | |

# Along the Way

**My Notes Along the Way**:

*Suggestions:*

- ✧ *Attractions*
- ✧ *Cities and towns traveled through*
- ✧ *Eats and treats*
- ✧ *Points of interest*
- ✧ *Routes followed*
- ✧ *Routes to avoid*
- ✧ *Scenic views*
- ✧ *Shopping*
- ✧ *Wildlife seen*
- ✧ *Anything else you experience along the way!*

# Day's End

| Stayed Overnight: | ❑ Campground   ❑ Cracker Barrel   ❑ Walmart   ❑ Other: |
|---|---|
| **Campground Name:** | Site #:          Cost: |
| **Campground Notes:** | ❑ Full Hookups   ❑ 50-amp   ❑ Showers   ❑ Laundry   ❑ RV Dump   ❑ Wi-Fi   ❑ Camp Store <br><br><br><br><br><br><br> *Noise:* ❑ Quiet ❑ Some ❑ Noisy • *Overall:* ❑ Poor ❑ Fair ❑ Good ❑ Excellent |
| **Overnight Parking Notes:** | <br><br><br> *Noise:* ❑ Quiet ❑ Some ❑ Noisy • *Overall:* ❑ Poor ❑ Fair ❑ Good ❑ Excellent |
| **Dinner:** | |
| **People Met Today:** | |

# Miscellaneous Notes

| Other Notes About Today's Journey: <br><br>*Suggestions:*<br><br>✧ *Things to see and do next time*<br>✧ *Weather conditions*<br>✧ *Anything else you want to remember!* | |
|---|---|

# The Journey

| Departure: | Date: | Time: | Holiday?  ❑ Yes ❑ No |
|---|---|---|---|
| **Departed From**: | | | |
| **Destination**: | | | |
| **Arrival**: | Time: | Hours Traveled: | |
| **Mileage**: | Start: | End: | Total: |
| **Planned Travel Routes**: | | | |

# Along the Way

| My Notes Along the Way:<br><br>*Suggestions:*<br><br>✧ *Attractions*<br>✧ *Cities and towns traveled through*<br>✧ *Eats and treats*<br>✧ *Points of interest*<br>✧ *Routes followed*<br>✧ *Routes to avoid*<br>✧ *Scenic views*<br>✧ *Shopping*<br>✧ *Wildlife seen*<br>✧ *Anything else you experience along the way!* | |
|---|---|

# Day's End

| Stayed Overnight: | ❑ Campground    ❑ Cracker Barrel    ❑ Walmart    ❑ Other: |
|---|---|
| **Campground Name:** | Site #:          Cost: |
| **Campground Notes:** | ❑ Full Hookups    ❑ 50-amp    ❑ Showers    ❑ Laundry    ❑ RV Dump    ❑ Wi-Fi    ❑ Camp Store<br><br><br><br><br><br>*Noise:* ❑ Quiet ❑ Some ❑ Noisy  ◆ *Overall:* ❑ Poor ❑ Fair ❑ Good ❑ Excellent |
| **Overnight Parking Notes:** | <br><br><br>*Noise:* ❑ Quiet ❑ Some ❑ Noisy  ◆ *Overall:* ❑ Poor ❑ Fair ❑ Good ❑ Excellent |
| **Dinner:** | |
| **People Met Today:** | |

# Miscellaneous Notes

| Other Notes About Today's Journey:<br><br>*Suggestions:*<br><br>✧ *Things to see and do next time*<br>✧ *Weather conditions*<br>✧ *Anything else you want to remember!* | |
|---|---|

# The Journey

| Departure: | Date: | Time: | Holiday?  ❏ Yes  ❏ No |
|---|---|---|---|
| **Departed From:** | | | |
| **Destination:** | | | |
| **Arrival:** | Time: | Hours Traveled: | |
| **Mileage:** | Start: | End: | Total: |
| **Planned Travel Routes:** | | | |

# Along the Way

| My Notes Along the Way: | |
|---|---|
| *Suggestions:* | |
| ✧ *Attractions* | |
| ✧ *Cities and towns traveled through* | |
| ✧ *Eats and treats* | |
| ✧ *Points of interest* | |
| ✧ *Routes followed* | |
| ✧ *Routes to avoid* | |
| ✧ *Scenic views* | |
| ✧ *Shopping* | |
| ✧ *Wildlife seen* | |
| ✧ *Anything else you experience along the way!* | |

# Day's End

| Stayed Overnight: | ❑ Campground    ❑ Cracker Barrel    ❑ Walmart    ❑ Other: |
|---|---|
| **Campground Name:** | Site #:                    Cost: |
| **Campground Notes:** | ❑ Full Hookups    ❑ 50-amp    ❑ Showers    ❑ Laundry    ❑ RV Dump    ❑ Wi-Fi    ❑ Camp Store<br><br><br><br><br><br>*Noise:* ❑ Quiet ❑ Some ❑ Noisy  •  *Overall:* ❑ Poor ❑ Fair ❑ Good ❑ Excellent |
| **Overnight Parking Notes:** | <br><br><br>*Noise:* ❑ Quiet ❑ Some ❑ Noisy  •  *Overall:* ❑ Poor ❑ Fair ❑ Good ❑ Excellent |
| **Dinner:** | |
| **People Met Today:** | |

# Miscellaneous Notes

| Other Notes About Today's Journey:<br><br>*Suggestions:*<br><br>✧  *Things to see and do next time*<br>✧  *Weather conditions*<br>✧  *Anything else you want to remember!* | |
|---|---|

# The Journey

| Departure: | Date: | | Time: | | Holiday?  ❏ Yes  ❏ No |
|---|---|---|---|---|---|
| **Departed From**: | | | | | |
| **Destination**: | | | | | |
| **Arrival**: | Time: | | Hours Traveled: | | |
| **Mileage**: | Start: | End: | | Total: | |
| **Planned Travel Routes**: | | | | | |

# Along the Way

**My Notes Along the Way**:

*Suggestions:*

◇ *Attractions*

◇ *Cities and towns traveled through*

◇ *Eats and treats*

◇ *Points of interest*

◇ *Routes followed*

◇ *Routes to avoid*

◇ *Scenic views*

◇ *Shopping*

◇ *Wildlife seen*

◇ *Anything else you experience along the way!*

# Day's End

| Stayed Overnight: | ❑ Campground ❑ Cracker Barrel ❑ Walmart ❑ Other: |
|---|---|
| **Campground Name:** | Site #: Cost: |
| **Campground Notes:** | ❑ Full Hookups ❑ 50-amp ❑ Showers ❑ Laundry ❑ RV Dump ❑ Wi-Fi ❑ Camp Store<br><br><br><br><br><br>*Noise:* ❑ Quiet ❑ Some ❑ Noisy ◆ *Overall:* ❑ Poor ❑ Fair ❑ Good ❑ Excellent |
| **Overnight Parking Notes:** | <br><br>*Noise:* ❑ Quiet ❑ Some ❑ Noisy ◆ *Overall:* ❑ Poor ❑ Fair ❑ Good ❑ Excellent |
| **Dinner:** | |
| **People Met Today:** | |

# Miscellaneous Notes

| Other Notes About Today's Journey:<br><br>*Suggestions:*<br><br>✧ *Things to see and do next time*<br>✧ *Weather conditions*<br>✧ *Anything else you want to remember!* | |
|---|---|

# The Journey

| Departure: | Date: | Time: | Holiday? ❑ Yes ❑ No |
|---|---|---|---|
| **Departed From**: | | | |
| **Destination**: | | | |
| **Arrival**: | Time: | Hours Traveled: | |
| **Mileage**: | Start: | End: | Total: |
| **Planned Travel Routes**: | | | |

# Along the Way

**My Notes Along the Way**:

*Suggestions:*

✦ *Attractions*
✦ *Cities and towns traveled through*
✦ *Eats and treats*
✦ *Points of interest*
✦ *Routes followed*
✦ *Routes to avoid*
✦ *Scenic views*
✦ *Shopping*
✦ *Wildlife seen*
✦ *Anything else you experience along the way!*

# Day's End

| Stayed Overnight: | ❑ Campground   ❑ Cracker Barrel   ❑ Walmart   ❑ Other: |
|---|---|
| **Campground Name:** | Site #:                    Cost: |
| **Campground Notes:** | ❑ Full Hookups   ❑ 50-amp   ❑ Showers   ❑ Laundry   ❑ RV Dump   ❑ Wi-Fi   ❑ Camp Store <br><br><br><br><br><br> *Noise:* ❑ Quiet ❑ Some ❑ Noisy  •  *Overall:* ❑ Poor ❑ Fair ❑ Good ❑ Excellent |
| **Overnight Parking Notes:** | <br><br> *Noise:* ❑ Quiet ❑ Some ❑ Noisy  •  *Overall:* ❑ Poor ❑ Fair ❑ Good ❑ Excellent |
| **Dinner:** | |
| **People Met Today:** | |

# Miscellaneous Notes

| Other Notes About Today's Journey:<br><br>*Suggestions:*<br><br>✧ *Things to see and do next time*<br>✧ *Weather conditions*<br>✧ *Anything else you want to remember!* | |
|---|---|

# The Journey

| Departure: | Date: | | Time: | | | Holiday? ❑ Yes ❑ No |
|---|---|---|---|---|---|---|
| **Departed From:** | | | | | | |
| **Destination:** | | | | | | |
| **Arrival:** | Time: | | | Hours Traveled: | | |
| **Mileage:** | Start: | | End: | | Total: | |
| **Planned Travel Routes:** | | | | | | |

# Along the Way

**My Notes Along the Way:**

*Suggestions:*

✧  *Attractions*

✧  *Cities and towns traveled through*

✧  *Eats and treats*

✧  *Points of interest*

✧  *Routes followed*

✧  *Routes to avoid*

✧  *Scenic views*

✧  *Shopping*

✧  *Wildlife seen*

✧  *Anything else you experience along the way!*

# Day's End

| Stayed Overnight: | ❑ Campground ❑ Cracker Barrel ❑ Walmart ❑ Other: |
|---|---|
| **Campground Name:** | Site #: Cost: |
| **Campground Notes:** | ❑ Full Hookups ❑ 50-amp ❑ Showers ❑ Laundry ❑ RV Dump ❑ Wi-Fi ❑ Camp Store <br><br><br><br><br><br> *Noise:* ❑ Quiet ❑ Some ❑ Noisy • *Overall:* ❑ Poor ❑ Fair ❑ Good ❑ Excellent |
| **Overnight Parking Notes:** | <br><br> *Noise:* ❑ Quiet ❑ Some ❑ Noisy • *Overall:* ❑ Poor ❑ Fair ❑ Good ❑ Excellent |
| **Dinner:** | |
| **People Met Today:** | |

# Miscellaneous Notes

| Other Notes About Today's Journey:<br><br>*Suggestions:*<br><br>✧ *Things to see and do next time*<br>✧ *Weather conditions*<br>✧ *Anything else you want to remember!* | |
|---|---|

# The Journey

| Departure: | Date:                    Time:                    Holiday?  ☐ Yes  ☐ No |
|---|---|
| **Departed From**: | |
| **Destination**: | |
| **Arrival**: | Time:                              Hours Traveled: |
| **Mileage**: | Start:                    End:                    Total: |
| **Planned Travel Routes**: | |

# Along the Way

| My Notes Along the Way: | |
|---|---|
| *Suggestions:* | |
| ✦ *Attractions* | |
| ✦ *Cities and towns traveled through* | |
| ✦ *Eats and treats* | |
| ✦ *Points of interest* | |
| ✦ *Routes followed* | |
| ✦ *Routes to avoid* | |
| ✦ *Scenic views* | |
| ✦ *Shopping* | |
| ✦ *Wildlife seen* | |
| ✦ *Anything else you experience along the way!* | |

# Day's End

| Stayed Overnight: | ❑ Campground  ❑ Cracker Barrel  ❑ Walmart  ❑ Other: | | |
|---|---|---|---|
| **Campground Name:** | | Site #: | Cost: |
| **Campground Notes:** | ❑ Full Hookups  ❑ 50-amp  ❑ Showers  ❑ Laundry  ❑ RV Dump  ❑ Wi-Fi  ❑ Camp Store | | |
| | | | |
| | *Noise:* ❑ Quiet  ❑ Some  ❑ Noisy  ◆ *Overall:* ❑ Poor  ❑ Fair  ❑ Good  ❑ Excellent | | |
| **Overnight Parking Notes:** | | | |
| | *Noise:* ❑ Quiet  ❑ Some  ❑ Noisy  ◆ *Overall:* ❑ Poor  ❑ Fair  ❑ Good  ❑ Excellent | | |
| **Dinner:** | | | |
| **People Met Today:** | | | |

# Miscellaneous Notes

| **Other Notes About Today's Journey:** *Suggestions:* ✧ *Things to see and do next time* ✧ *Weather conditions* ✧ *Anything else you want to remember!* | |
|---|---|

# The Journey

| Departure: | Date: | Time: | Holiday? ☐ Yes ☐ No |
|---|---|---|---|
| **Departed From:** | | | |
| **Destination:** | | | |
| **Arrival:** | Time: | Hours Traveled: | |
| **Mileage:** | Start: | End: | Total: |
| **Planned Travel Routes:** | | | |

# Along the Way

| My Notes Along the Way:<br><br>*Suggestions:*<br><br>✧ *Attractions*<br>✧ *Cities and towns traveled through*<br>✧ *Eats and treats*<br>✧ *Points of interest*<br>✧ *Routes followed*<br>✧ *Routes to avoid*<br>✧ *Scenic views*<br>✧ *Shopping*<br>✧ *Wildlife seen*<br>✧ *Anything else you experience along the way!* | |
|---|---|

# Day's End

| Stayed Overnight: | ❑ Campground  ❑ Cracker Barrel  ❑ Walmart  ❑ Other: |
|---|---|
| **Campground Name:** | Site #:           Cost: |
| **Campground Notes:** | ❑ Full Hookups  ❑ 50-amp  ❑ Showers  ❑ Laundry  ❑ RV Dump  ❑ Wi-Fi  ❑ Camp Store<br><br><br><br><br><br>*Noise:* ❑ Quiet ❑ Some ❑ Noisy  •  *Overall:* ❑ Poor ❑ Fair ❑ Good ❑ Excellent |
| **Overnight Parking Notes:** | <br><br>*Noise:* ❑ Quiet ❑ Some ❑ Noisy  •  *Overall:* ❑ Poor ❑ Fair ❑ Good ❑ Excellent |
| **Dinner:** | |
| **People Met Today:** | |

# Miscellaneous Notes

| Other Notes About Today's Journey:<br><br>*Suggestions:*<br><br>✧ *Things to see and do next time*<br>✧ *Weather conditions*<br>✧ *Anything else you want to remember!* | |
|---|---|

# The Journey

| Departure: | Date: | Time: | Holiday? ❑ Yes ❑ No |
|---|---|---|---|
| **Departed From**: | | | |
| **Destination**: | | | |
| **Arrival**: | Time: | Hours Traveled: | |
| **Mileage**: | Start: | End: | Total: |
| **Planned Travel Routes**: | | | |

# Along the Way

| **My Notes Along the Way**:<br><br>*Suggestions:*<br><br>✧ *Attractions*<br>✧ *Cities and towns traveled through*<br>✧ *Eats and treats*<br>✧ *Points of interest*<br>✧ *Routes followed*<br>✧ *Routes to avoid*<br>✧ *Scenic views*<br>✧ *Shopping*<br>✧ *Wildlife seen*<br>✧ *Anything else you experience along the way!* | |
|---|---|

# Day's End

| | |
|---|---|
| **Stayed Overnight:** | ❏ Campground  ❏ Cracker Barrel  ❏ Walmart  ❏ Other: |
| **Campground Name:** | Site #:          Cost: |
| **Campground Notes:** | ❏ Full Hookups  ❏ 50-amp  ❏ Showers  ❏ Laundry  ❏ RV Dump  ❏ Wi-Fi  ❏ Camp Store |
| | |
| | *Noise:* ❏ Quiet  ❏ Some  ❏ Noisy  ◆ *Overall:* ❏ Poor  ❏ Fair  ❏ Good  ❏ Excellent |
| **Overnight Parking Notes:** | |
| | *Noise:* ❏ Quiet  ❏ Some  ❏ Noisy  ◆ *Overall:* ❏ Poor  ❏ Fair  ❏ Good  ❏ Excellent |
| **Dinner:** | |
| **People Met Today:** | |

# Miscellaneous Notes

| | |
|---|---|
| **Other Notes About Today's Journey:**  *Suggestions:*  ✧ *Things to see and do next time*  ✧ *Weather conditions*  ✧ *Anything else you want to remember!* | |

# The Journey

| Departure: | Date: | | Time: | | Holiday? ❑ Yes ❑ No |
|---|---|---|---|---|---|
| **Departed From:** | | | | | |
| **Destination:** | | | | | |
| **Arrival:** | Time: | | Hours Traveled: | | |
| **Mileage:** | Start: | End: | | Total: | |
| **Planned Travel Routes:** | | | | | |

# Along the Way

**My Notes Along the Way:**

*Suggestions:*

✧  *Attractions*

✧  *Cities and towns traveled through*

✧  *Eats and treats*

✧  *Points of interest*

✧  *Routes followed*

✧  *Routes to avoid*

✧  *Scenic views*

✧  *Shopping*

✧  *Wildlife seen*

✧  *Anything else you experience along the way!*

# Day's End

| Stayed Overnight: | ❏ Campground    ❏ Cracker Barrel    ❏ Walmart    ❏ Other: |
|---|---|
| Campground Name: | Site #:         Cost: |
| Campground Notes: | ❏ Full Hookups    ❏ 50-amp    ❏ Showers    ❏ Laundry    ❏ RV Dump    ❏ Wi-Fi    ❏ Camp Store <br><br><br><br><br><br><br><br>*Noise:* ❏ Quiet  ❏ Some  ❏ Noisy  •  *Overall:* ❏ Poor  ❏ Fair  ❏ Good  ❏ Excellent |
| Overnight Parking Notes: | <br><br><br>*Noise:* ❏ Quiet  ❏ Some  ❏ Noisy  •  *Overall:* ❏ Poor  ❏ Fair  ❏ Good  ❏ Excellent |
| Dinner: | |
| People Met Today: | |

# Miscellaneous Notes

| Other Notes About Today's Journey: <br><br>*Suggestions:* <br><br>✧ *Things to see and do next time* <br>✧ *Weather conditions* <br>✧ *Anything else you want to remember!* | |
|---|---|

# The Journey

| Departure: | Date: | Time: | Holiday? ☐ Yes ☐ No |
|---|---|---|---|
| **Departed From**: | | | |
| **Destination**: | | | |
| **Arrival**: | Time: | Hours Traveled: | |
| **Mileage**: | Start: | End: | Total: |
| **Planned Travel Routes**: | | | |

# Along the Way

**My Notes Along the Way**:

*Suggestions:*

✦ *Attractions*

✦ *Cities and towns traveled through*

✦ *Eats and treats*

✦ *Points of interest*

✦ *Routes followed*

✦ *Routes to avoid*

✦ *Scenic views*

✦ *Shopping*

✦ *Wildlife seen*

✦ *Anything else you experience along the way!*

# Day's End

| Stayed Overnight: | ❑ Campground   ❑ Cracker Barrel   ❑ Walmart   ❑ Other: |
|---|---|
| Campground Name: | Site #:          Cost: |
| Campground Notes: | ❑ Full Hookups   ❑ 50-amp   ❑ Showers   ❑ Laundry   ❑ RV Dump   ❑ Wi-Fi   ❑ Camp Store |
| | |
| | *Noise:* ❑ Quiet ❑ Some ❑ Noisy  •  *Overall:* ❑ Poor ❑ Fair ❑ Good ❑ Excellent |
| Overnight Parking Notes: | |
| | *Noise:* ❑ Quiet ❑ Some ❑ Noisy  •  *Overall:* ❑ Poor ❑ Fair ❑ Good ❑ Excellent |
| Dinner: | |
| People Met Today: | |

# Miscellaneous Notes

| Other Notes About Today's Journey:  *Suggestions:*  ✧ *Things to see and do next time*  ✧ *Weather conditions*  ✧ *Anything else you want to remember!* | |
|---|---|

# The Journey

| Departure: | Date: | Time: | Holiday? ☐ Yes ☐ No |
|---|---|---|---|
| **Departed From:** | | | |
| **Destination:** | | | |
| **Arrival:** | Time: | Hours Traveled: | |
| **Mileage:** | Start: | End: | Total: |
| **Planned Travel Routes:** | | | |

# Along the Way

**My Notes Along the Way:**

*Suggestions:*

- ✧ *Attractions*
- ✧ *Cities and towns traveled through*
- ✧ *Eats and treats*
- ✧ *Points of interest*
- ✧ *Routes followed*
- ✧ *Routes to avoid*
- ✧ *Scenic views*
- ✧ *Shopping*
- ✧ *Wildlife seen*
- ✧ *Anything else you experience along the way!*

# Day's End

| Stayed Overnight: | ❑ Campground    ❑ Cracker Barrel    ❑ Walmart    ❑ Other: |
|---|---|
| **Campground Name:** | Site #:          Cost: |
| **Campground Notes:** | ❑ Full Hookups  ❑ 50-amp  ❑ Showers  ❑ Laundry  ❑ RV Dump  ❑ Wi-Fi  ❑ Camp Store |
| | |
| | *Noise:* ❑ Quiet ❑ Some ❑ Noisy  •  *Overall:* ❑ Poor ❑ Fair ❑ Good ❑ Excellent |
| **Overnight Parking Notes:** | |
| | *Noise:* ❑ Quiet ❑ Some ❑ Noisy  •  *Overall:* ❑ Poor ❑ Fair ❑ Good ❑ Excellent |
| **Dinner:** | |
| **People Met Today:** | |

# Miscellaneous Notes

| **Other Notes About Today's Journey:**  *Suggestions:*  ✧  *Things to see and do next time*  ✧  *Weather conditions*  ✧  *Anything else you want to remember!* | |
|---|---|

# The Journey

| Departure: | Date: | Time: | Holiday? ☐ Yes ☐ No |
|---|---|---|---|
| **Departed From:** | | | |
| **Destination:** | | | |
| **Arrival:** | Time: | Hours Traveled: | |
| **Mileage:** | Start: | End: | Total: |
| **Planned Travel Routes:** | | | |

# Along the Way

| My Notes Along the Way:<br><br>*Suggestions:*<br><br>✧ *Attractions*<br>✧ *Cities and towns traveled through*<br>✧ *Eats and treats*<br>✧ *Points of interest*<br>✧ *Routes followed*<br>✧ *Routes to avoid*<br>✧ *Scenic views*<br>✧ *Shopping*<br>✧ *Wildlife seen*<br>✧ *Anything else you experience along the way!* | |
|---|---|

# Day's End

| | |
|---|---|
| **Stayed Overnight:** | ❑ Campground  ❑ Cracker Barrel  ❑ Walmart  ❑ Other: |
| **Campground Name:** | Site #:        Cost: |
| **Campground Notes:** | ❑ Full Hookups  ❑ 50-amp  ❑ Showers  ❑ Laundry  ❑ RV Dump  ❑ Wi-Fi  ❑ Camp Store <br><br><br><br><br> *Noise:* ❑ Quiet  ❑ Some  ❑ Noisy  ◆ *Overall:* ❑ Poor  ❑ Fair  ❑ Good  ❑ Excellent |
| **Overnight Parking Notes:** | <br><br> *Noise:* ❑ Quiet  ❑ Some  ❑ Noisy  ◆ *Overall:* ❑ Poor  ❑ Fair  ❑ Good  ❑ Excellent |
| **Dinner:** | |
| **People Met Today:** | |

# Miscellaneous Notes

| | |
|---|---|
| **Other Notes About Today's Journey:** <br><br> *Suggestions:* <br><br> ✧ *Things to see and do next time* <br> ✧ *Weather conditions* <br> ✧ *Anything else you want to remember!* | |

# The Journey

| Departure: | Date: | | Time: | | Holiday? ❏ Yes ❏ No |
|---|---|---|---|---|---|
| **Departed From**: | | | | | |
| **Destination**: | | | | | |
| **Arrival**: | Time: | | Hours Traveled: | | |
| **Mileage**: | Start: | End: | | Total: | |
| **Planned Travel Routes**: | | | | | |

# Along the Way

| **My Notes Along the Way**:<br><br>*Suggestions:*<br><br>✧ *Attractions*<br>✧ *Cities and towns traveled through*<br>✧ *Eats and treats*<br>✧ *Points of interest*<br>✧ *Routes followed*<br>✧ *Routes to avoid*<br>✧ *Scenic views*<br>✧ *Shopping*<br>✧ *Wildlife seen*<br>✧ *Anything else you experience along the way!* | |
|---|---|

# Day's End

| Stayed Overnight: | ❏ Campground    ❏ Cracker Barrel    ❏ Walmart    ❏ Other: |
|---|---|
| **Campground Name:** | Site #:      Cost: |
| **Campground Notes:** | ❏ Full Hookups   ❏ 50-amp   ❏ Showers   ❏ Laundry   ❏ RV Dump   ❏ Wi-Fi   ❏ Camp Store<br><br><br><br><br><br>*Noise:* ❏ Quiet   ❏ Some   ❏ Noisy   •   *Overall:* ❏ Poor   ❏ Fair   ❏ Good   ❏ Excellent |
| **Overnight Parking Notes:** | <br><br>*Noise:* ❏ Quiet   ❏ Some   ❏ Noisy   •   *Overall:* ❏ Poor   ❏ Fair   ❏ Good   ❏ Excellent |
| **Dinner:** | |
| **People Met Today:** | |

# Miscellaneous Notes

| **Other Notes About Today's Journey:**<br><br>*Suggestions:*<br><br>  ✧   *Things to see and do next time*<br>  ✧   *Weather conditions*<br>  ✧   *Anything else you want to remember!* | |
|---|---|

# The Journey

| Departure: | Date: | Time: | Holiday? ❏ Yes ❏ No |
|---|---|---|---|
| **Departed From:** | | | |
| **Destination:** | | | |
| **Arrival:** | Time: | Hours Traveled: | |
| **Mileage:** | Start: | End: | Total: |
| **Planned Travel Routes:** | | | |

# Along the Way

**My Notes Along the Way:**

*Suggestions:*

- ✧ *Attractions*
- ✧ *Cities and towns traveled through*
- ✧ *Eats and treats*
- ✧ *Points of interest*
- ✧ *Routes followed*
- ✧ *Routes to avoid*
- ✧ *Scenic views*
- ✧ *Shopping*
- ✧ *Wildlife seen*
- ✧ *Anything else you experience along the way!*

# Day's End

| Stayed Overnight: | ❑ Campground  ❑ Cracker Barrel  ❑ Walmart  ❑ Other: |
|---|---|
| **Campground Name:** | Site #:          Cost: |
| **Campground Notes:** | ❑ Full Hookups  ❑ 50-amp  ❑ Showers  ❑ Laundry  ❑ RV Dump  ❑ Wi-Fi  ❑ Camp Store <br><br><br><br>*Noise:* ❑ Quiet ❑ Some ❑ Noisy  ⬥ *Overall:* ❑ Poor ❑ Fair ❑ Good ❑ Excellent |
| **Overnight Parking Notes:** | <br><br>*Noise:* ❑ Quiet ❑ Some ❑ Noisy  ⬥ *Overall:* ❑ Poor ❑ Fair ❑ Good ❑ Excellent |
| **Dinner:** | |
| **People Met Today:** | |

# Miscellaneous Notes

| **Other Notes About Today's Journey:** <br><br> *Suggestions:* <br><br> ✧ *Things to see and do next time* <br> ✧ *Weather conditions* <br> ✧ *Anything else you want to remember!* | |
|---|---|

# The Journey

| Departure: | Date: | | Time: | | Holiday? ❑ Yes ❑ No |
|---|---|---|---|---|---|
| **Departed From**: | | | | | |
| **Destination**: | | | | | |
| **Arrival**: | Time: | | Hours Traveled: | | |
| **Mileage**: | Start: | End: | | Total: | |
| **Planned Travel Routes**: | | | | | |

# Along the Way

**My Notes Along the Way**:

*Suggestions:*

 ✧  *Attractions*

 ✧  *Cities and towns traveled through*

 ✧  *Eats and treats*

 ✧  *Points of interest*

 ✧  *Routes followed*

 ✧  *Routes to avoid*

 ✧  *Scenic views*

 ✧  *Shopping*

 ✧  *Wildlife seen*

 ✧  *Anything else you experience along the way!*

# Day's End

| Stayed Overnight: | ❑ Campground   ❑ Cracker Barrel   ❑ Walmart   ❑ Other: |
|---|---|
| **Campground Name:** | Site #:          Cost: |
| **Campground Notes:** | ❑ Full Hookups   ❑ 50-amp   ❑ Showers   ❑ Laundry   ❑ RV Dump   ❑ Wi-Fi   ❑ Camp Store <br><br><br><br><br><br> *Noise:* ❑ Quiet  ❑ Some  ❑ Noisy  •  *Overall:* ❑ Poor  ❑ Fair  ❑ Good  ❑ Excellent |
| **Overnight Parking Notes:** | <br><br> *Noise:* ❑ Quiet  ❑ Some  ❑ Noisy  •  *Overall:* ❑ Poor  ❑ Fair  ❑ Good  ❑ Excellent |
| **Dinner:** | |
| **People Met Today:** | |

# Miscellaneous Notes

| Other Notes About Today's Journey: <br><br> *Suggestions:* <br><br> ✧ *Things to see and do next time* <br> ✧ *Weather conditions* <br> ✧ *Anything else you want to remember!* | |
|---|---|

# The Journey

| Departure: | Date: | Time: | Holiday?  ☐ Yes ☐ No |
|---|---|---|---|
| Departed From: | | | |
| Destination: | | | |
| Arrival: | Time: | Hours Traveled: | |
| Mileage: | Start: | End: | Total: |
| Planned Travel Routes: | | | |

# Along the Way

**My Notes Along the Way:**

*Suggestions:*

- ✧ Attractions
- ✧ Cities and towns traveled through
- ✧ Eats and treats
- ✧ Points of interest
- ✧ Routes followed
- ✧ Routes to avoid
- ✧ Scenic views
- ✧ Shopping
- ✧ Wildlife seen
- ✧ Anything else you experience along the way!

# Day's End

| | |
|---|---|
| **Stayed Overnight:** | ❑ Campground  ❑ Cracker Barrel  ❑ Walmart  ❑ Other: |
| **Campground Name:** | Site #:          Cost: |
| **Campground Notes:** | ❑ Full Hookups  ❑ 50-amp  ❑ Showers  ❑ Laundry  ❑ RV Dump  ❑ Wi-Fi  ❑ Camp Store<br><br><br><br><br><br>*Noise:* ❑ Quiet  ❑ Some  ❑ Noisy  •  *Overall:* ❑ Poor  ❑ Fair  ❑ Good  ❑ Excellent |
| **Overnight Parking Notes:** | <br><br><br>*Noise:* ❑ Quiet  ❑ Some  ❑ Noisy  •  *Overall:* ❑ Poor  ❑ Fair  ❑ Good  ❑ Excellent |
| **Dinner:** | |
| **People Met Today:** | |

# Miscellaneous Notes

| | |
|---|---|
| **Other Notes About Today's Journey:**<br><br>*Suggestions:*<br><br>✧  *Things to see and do next time*<br>✧  *Weather conditions*<br>✧  *Anything else you want to remember!* | |

# The Journey

| Departure: | Date: | Time: | Holiday? ☐ Yes ☐ No |
|---|---|---|---|
| **Departed From:** | | | |
| **Destination:** | | | |
| **Arrival:** | Time: | Hours Traveled: | |
| **Mileage:** | Start: | End: | Total: |
| **Planned Travel Routes:** | | | |

# Along the Way

| **My Notes Along the Way:** *Suggestions:* ✧ *Attractions* ✧ *Cities and towns traveled through* ✧ *Eats and treats* ✧ *Points of interest* ✧ *Routes followed* ✧ *Routes to avoid* ✧ *Scenic views* ✧ *Shopping* ✧ *Wildlife seen* ✧ *Anything else you experience along the way!* | |
|---|---|

# Day's End

| Stayed Overnight: | ❑ Campground   ❑ Cracker Barrel   ❑ Walmart   ❑ Other: |
|---|---|
| **Campground Name:** | Site #:                    Cost: |
| **Campground Notes:** | ❑ Full Hookups   ❑ 50-amp   ❑ Showers   ❑ Laundry   ❑ RV Dump   ❑ Wi-Fi   ❑ Camp Store<br><br><br><br><br><br><br>*Noise:* ❑ Quiet ❑ Some ❑ Noisy ◆ *Overall:* ❑ Poor ❑ Fair ❑ Good ❑ Excellent |
| **Overnight Parking Notes:** | <br><br><br>*Noise:* ❑ Quiet ❑ Some ❑ Noisy ◆ *Overall:* ❑ Poor ❑ Fair ❑ Good ❑ Excellent |
| **Dinner:** | |
| **People Met Today:** | |

# Miscellaneous Notes

| Other Notes About Today's Journey:<br><br>*Suggestions:*<br><br>✧ *Things to see and do next time*<br>✧ *Weather conditions*<br>✧ *Anything else you want to remember!* | |
|---|---|

# The Journey

| Departure: | Date: | Time: | Holiday?  ❏ Yes ❏ No |
|---|---|---|---|
| **Departed From**: | | | |
| **Destination**: | | | |
| **Arrival**: | Time: | Hours Traveled: | |
| **Mileage**: | Start: | End: | Total: |
| **Planned Travel Routes**: | | | |

# Along the Way

**My Notes Along the Way:**

*Suggestions:*

✧  *Attractions*

✧  *Cities and towns traveled through*

✧  *Eats and treats*

✧  *Points of interest*

✧  *Routes followed*

✧  *Routes to avoid*

✧  *Scenic views*

✧  *Shopping*

✧  *Wildlife seen*

✧  *Anything else you experience along the way!*

# Day's End

| Stayed Overnight: | ❏ Campground ❏ Cracker Barrel ❏ Walmart ❏ Other: |
|---|---|
| **Campground Name:** | Site #:     Cost: |
| **Campground Notes:** | ❏ Full Hookups ❏ 50-amp ❏ Showers ❏ Laundry ❏ RV Dump ❏ Wi-Fi ❏ Camp Store <br><br><br><br><br><br> *Noise:* ❏ Quiet ❏ Some ❏ Noisy • *Overall:* ❏ Poor ❏ Fair ❏ Good ❏ Excellent |
| **Overnight Parking Notes:** | <br><br> *Noise:* ❏ Quiet ❏ Some ❏ Noisy • *Overall:* ❏ Poor ❏ Fair ❏ Good ❏ Excellent |
| **Dinner:** | |
| **People Met Today:** | |

# Miscellaneous Notes

| Other Notes About Today's Journey: <br><br> *Suggestions:* <br><br> ✧ *Things to see and do next time* <br> ✧ *Weather conditions* <br> ✧ *Anything else you want to remember!* | |
|---|---|

# The Journey

| Departure: | Date: | Time: | Holiday? ❑ Yes ❑ No |
|---|---|---|---|
| **Departed From**: | | | |
| **Destination**: | | | |
| **Arrival**: | Time: | Hours Traveled: | |
| **Mileage**: | Start: | End: | Total: |
| **Planned Travel Routes**: | | | |

# Along the Way

| My Notes Along the Way:<br><br>*Suggestions:*<br><br>✧  *Attractions*<br>✧  *Cities and towns traveled through*<br>✧  *Eats and treats*<br>✧  *Points of interest*<br>✧  *Routes followed*<br>✧  *Routes to avoid*<br>✧  *Scenic views*<br>✧  *Shopping*<br>✧  *Wildlife seen*<br>✧  *Anything else you experience along the way!* | |
|---|---|

# Day's End

| Stayed Overnight: | ❑ Campground  ❑ Cracker Barrel  ❑ Walmart  ❑ Other: |
|---|---|
| **Campground Name:** | Site #:          Cost: |
| **Campground Notes:** | ❑ Full Hookups  ❑ 50-amp  ❑ Showers  ❑ Laundry  ❑ RV Dump  ❑ Wi-Fi  ❑ Camp Store<br><br><br><br>*Noise:* ❑ Quiet ❑ Some ❑ Noisy  •  *Overall:* ❑ Poor ❑ Fair ❑ Good ❑ Excellent |
| **Overnight Parking Notes:** | <br><br>*Noise:* ❑ Quiet ❑ Some ❑ Noisy  •  *Overall:* ❑ Poor ❑ Fair ❑ Good ❑ Excellent |
| **Dinner:** | |
| **People Met Today:** | |

# Miscellaneous Notes

| **Other Notes About Today's Journey:**<br><br>*Suggestions:*<br><br>✧ *Things to see and do next time*<br>✧ *Weather conditions*<br>✧ *Anything else you want to remember!* | |
|---|---|

# The Journey

| Departure: | Date: | Time: | Holiday?  ☐ Yes  ☐ No |
|---|---|---|---|
| **Departed From**: | | | |
| **Destination**: | | | |
| **Arrival**: | Time: | Hours Traveled: | |
| **Mileage**: | Start: | End: | Total: |
| **Planned Travel Routes**: | | | |

# Along the Way

**My Notes Along the Way:**

*Suggestions:*

- ✧ *Attractions*
- ✧ *Cities and towns traveled through*
- ✧ *Eats and treats*
- ✧ *Points of interest*
- ✧ *Routes followed*
- ✧ *Routes to avoid*
- ✧ *Scenic views*
- ✧ *Shopping*
- ✧ *Wildlife seen*
- ✧ *Anything else you experience along the way!*

# Day's End

| Stayed Overnight: | ❏ Campground   ❏ Cracker Barrel   ❏ Walmart   ❏ Other: |
|---|---|
| Campground Name: | Site #:          Cost: |
| Campground Notes: | ❏ Full Hookups   ❏ 50-amp   ❏ Showers   ❏ Laundry   ❏ RV Dump   ❏ Wi-Fi   ❏ Camp Store |
| | |
| | *Noise:* ❏ Quiet ❏ Some ❏ Noisy  ⬩ *Overall:* ❏ Poor ❏ Fair ❏ Good ❏ Excellent |
| Overnight Parking Notes: | |
| | *Noise:* ❏ Quiet ❏ Some ❏ Noisy  ⬩ *Overall:* ❏ Poor ❏ Fair ❏ Good ❏ Excellent |
| Dinner: | |
| People Met Today: | |

# Miscellaneous Notes

| Other Notes About Today's Journey:<br><br>*Suggestions:*<br><br>✧ *Things to see and do next time*<br>✧ *Weather conditions*<br>✧ *Anything else you want to remember!* | |
|---|---|

# The Journey

| Departure: | Date: | Time: | Holiday?  ☐ Yes ☐ No |
|---|---|---|---|
| **Departed From:** | | | |
| **Destination:** | | | |
| **Arrival:** | Time: | Hours Traveled: | |
| **Mileage:** | Start: | End: | Total: |
| **Planned Travel Routes:** | | | |

# Along the Way

| My Notes Along the Way:  *Suggestions:*  ✧ *Attractions*  ✧ *Cities and towns traveled through*  ✧ *Eats and treats*  ✧ *Points of interest*  ✧ *Routes followed*  ✧ *Routes to avoid*  ✧ *Scenic views*  ✧ *Shopping*  ✧ *Wildlife seen*  ✧ *Anything else you experience along the way!* | |
|---|---|

# Day's End

| Stayed Overnight: | ❑ Campground   ❑ Cracker Barrel   ❑ Walmart   ❑ Other: | | |
|---|---|---|---|
| **Campground Name:** | | Site #: | Cost: |
| **Campground Notes:** | ❑ Full Hookups   ❑ 50-amp   ❑ Showers   ❑ Laundry   ❑ RV Dump   ❑ Wi-Fi   ❑ Camp Store | | |
| | *Noise:* ❑ Quiet  ❑ Some  ❑ Noisy  ⬩ *Overall:* ❑ Poor  ❑ Fair  ❑ Good  ❑ Excellent | | |
| **Overnight Parking Notes:** | | | |
| | *Noise:* ❑ Quiet  ❑ Some  ❑ Noisy  ⬩ *Overall:* ❑ Poor  ❑ Fair  ❑ Good  ❑ Excellent | | |
| **Dinner:** | | | |
| **People Met Today:** | | | |

# Miscellaneous Notes

| Other Notes About Today's Journey: *Suggestions:*  ✧ *Things to see and do next time*  ✧ *Weather conditions*  ✧ *Anything else you want to remember!* | |
|---|---|

# The Journey

| Departure: | Date: | | Time: | Holiday? ☐ Yes ☐ No |
|---|---|---|---|---|
| **Departed From**: | | | | |
| **Destination**: | | | | |
| **Arrival**: | Time: | | Hours Traveled: | |
| **Mileage**: | Start: | End: | Total: | |
| **Planned Travel Routes**: | | | | |

# Along the Way

**My Notes Along the Way**:

*Suggestions:*

- ✧ *Attractions*
- ✧ *Cities and towns traveled through*
- ✧ *Eats and treats*
- ✧ *Points of interest*
- ✧ *Routes followed*
- ✧ *Routes to avoid*
- ✧ *Scenic views*
- ✧ *Shopping*
- ✧ *Wildlife seen*
- ✧ *Anything else you experience along the way!*

# Day's End

| Stayed Overnight: | ❑ Campground ❑ Cracker Barrel ❑ Walmart ❑ Other: |
|---|---|
| **Campground Name:** | Site #: Cost: |
| **Campground Notes:** | ❑ Full Hookups ❑ 50-amp ❑ Showers ❑ Laundry ❑ RV Dump ❑ Wi-Fi ❑ Camp Store <br><br><br><br><br> *Noise:* ❑ Quiet ❑ Some ❑ Noisy • *Overall:* ❑ Poor ❑ Fair ❑ Good ❑ Excellent |
| **Overnight Parking Notes:** | <br><br> *Noise:* ❑ Quiet ❑ Some ❑ Noisy • *Overall:* ❑ Poor ❑ Fair ❑ Good ❑ Excellent |
| **Dinner:** | |
| **People Met Today:** | |

# Miscellaneous Notes

| Other Notes About Today's Journey: <br><br> *Suggestions:* <br><br> ✧ *Things to see and do next time* <br> ✧ *Weather conditions* <br> ✧ *Anything else you want to remember!* | |
|---|---|

# The Journey

| Departure: | Date: | | Time: | | Holiday? ❑ Yes ❑ No |
|---|---|---|---|---|---|
| **Departed From:** | | | | | |
| **Destination:** | | | | | |
| **Arrival:** | Time: | | Hours Traveled: | | |
| **Mileage:** | Start: | End: | | Total: | |
| **Planned Travel Routes:** | | | | | |

# Along the Way

| **My Notes Along the Way:** | |
|---|---|
| *Suggestions:* | |
| ✧ *Attractions* | |
| ✧ *Cities and towns traveled through* | |
| ✧ *Eats and treats* | |
| ✧ *Points of interest* | |
| ✧ *Routes followed* | |
| ✧ *Routes to avoid* | |
| ✧ *Scenic views* | |
| ✧ *Shopping* | |
| ✧ *Wildlife seen* | |
| ✧ *Anything else you experience along the way!* | |

# Day's End

| | |
|---|---|
| **Stayed Overnight:** | ❏ Campground    ❏ Cracker Barrel    ❏ Walmart    ❏ Other: |
| **Campground Name:** | Site #:              Cost: |
| **Campground Notes:** | ❏ Full Hookups   ❏ 50-amp   ❏ Showers   ❏ Laundry   ❏ RV Dump   ❏ Wi-Fi  ❏ Camp Store <br><br><br><br><br><br> *Noise:* ❏ Quiet ❏ Some ❏ Noisy  •  *Overall:* ❏ Poor ❏ Fair ❏ Good ❏ Excellent |
| **Overnight Parking Notes:** | <br><br><br> *Noise:* ❏ Quiet ❏ Some ❏ Noisy  •  *Overall:* ❏ Poor ❏ Fair ❏ Good ❏ Excellent |
| **Dinner:** | |
| **People Met Today:** | |

# Miscellaneous Notes

| | |
|---|---|
| **Other Notes About Today's Journey:** <br><br> *Suggestions:* <br><br> ✧ *Things to see and do next time* <br> ✧ *Weather conditions* <br> ✧ *Anything else you want to remember!* | |

# The Journey

| Departure: | Date: | Time: | Holiday? ❑ Yes ❑ No |
|---|---|---|---|
| **Departed From:** | | | |
| **Destination:** | | | |
| **Arrival:** | Time: | Hours Traveled: | |
| **Mileage:** | Start: | End: | Total: |
| **Planned Travel Routes:** | | | |

# Along the Way

| **My Notes Along the Way:** | |
|---|---|
| *Suggestions:* | |
| ✧  *Attractions* | |
| ✧  *Cities and towns traveled through* | |
| ✧  *Eats and treats* | |
| ✧  *Points of interest* | |
| ✧  *Routes followed* | |
| ✧  *Routes to avoid* | |
| ✧  *Scenic views* | |
| ✧  *Shopping* | |
| ✧  *Wildlife seen* | |
| ✧  *Anything else you experience along the way!* | |

# Day's End

| | |
|---|---|
| **Stayed Overnight:** | ❑ Campground   ❑ Cracker Barrel   ❑ Walmart   ❑ Other: |
| **Campground Name:** | Site #:          Cost: |
| **Campground Notes:** | ❑ Full Hookups   ❑ 50-amp   ❑ Showers   ❑ Laundry   ❑ RV Dump   ❑ Wi-Fi   ❑ Camp Store <br><br><br><br><br><br> *Noise:* ❑ Quiet ❑ Some ❑ Noisy  ♦ *Overall:* ❑ Poor ❑ Fair ❑ Good ❑ Excellent |
| **Overnight Parking Notes:** | <br><br><br> *Noise:* ❑ Quiet ❑ Some ❑ Noisy  ♦ *Overall:* ❑ Poor ❑ Fair ❑ Good ❑ Excellent |
| **Dinner:** | |
| **People Met Today:** | |

# Miscellaneous Notes

| | |
|---|---|
| **Other Notes About Today's Journey:** <br><br> *Suggestions:* <br><br> ✧ *Things to see and do next time* <br> ✧ *Weather conditions* <br> ✧ *Anything else you want to remember!* | |

# The Journey

| Departure: | Date: | Time: | Holiday? ☐ Yes ☐ No |
|---|---|---|---|
| **Departed From**: | | | |
| **Destination**: | | | |
| **Arrival**: | Time: | Hours Traveled: | |
| **Mileage**: | Start: | End: | Total: |
| **Planned Travel Routes**: | | | |

# Along the Way

**My Notes Along the Way:**

*Suggestions:*

✧ *Attractions*

✧ *Cities and towns traveled through*

✧ *Eats and treats*

✧ *Points of interest*

✧ *Routes followed*

✧ *Routes to avoid*

✧ *Scenic views*

✧ *Shopping*

✧ *Wildlife seen*

✧ *Anything else you experience along the way!*

# Day's End

| Stayed Overnight: | ❏ Campground   ❏ Cracker Barrel   ❏ Walmart   ❏ Other: |
|---|---|
| Campground Name: | Site #:          Cost: |
| Campground Notes: | ❏ Full Hookups  ❏ 50-amp  ❏ Showers  ❏ Laundry  ❏ RV Dump  ❏ Wi-Fi  ❏ Camp Store <br><br><br><br><br><br> *Noise:* ❏ Quiet ❏ Some ❏ Noisy • *Overall:* ❏ Poor ❏ Fair ❏ Good ❏ Excellent |
| Overnight Parking Notes: | <br><br> *Noise:* ❏ Quiet ❏ Some ❏ Noisy • *Overall:* ❏ Poor ❏ Fair ❏ Good ❏ Excellent |
| Dinner: | |
| People Met Today: | |

# Miscellaneous Notes

| Other Notes About Today's Journey: <br><br> *Suggestions:* <br><br> ✧ *Things to see and do next time* <br> ✧ *Weather conditions* <br> ✧ *Anything else you want to remember!* | |
|---|---|

# The Journey

| Departure: | Date: | Time: | Holiday? ☐ Yes ☐ No |
|---|---|---|---|
| **Departed From:** | | | |
| **Destination:** | | | |
| **Arrival:** | Time: | Hours Traveled: | |
| **Mileage:** | Start: | End: | Total: |
| **Planned Travel Routes:** | | | |

# Along the Way

| My Notes Along the Way:<br><br>*Suggestions:*<br><br>✧ *Attractions*<br>✧ *Cities and towns traveled through*<br>✧ *Eats and treats*<br>✧ *Points of interest*<br>✧ *Routes followed*<br>✧ *Routes to avoid*<br>✧ *Scenic views*<br>✧ *Shopping*<br>✧ *Wildlife seen*<br>✧ *Anything else you experience along the way!* | |
|---|---|

# Day's End

| Stayed Overnight: | ❑ Campground   ❑ Cracker Barrel   ❑ Walmart   ❑ Other: | | | | | |
|---|---|---|---|---|---|---|
| **Campground Name:** | | | | Site #: | | Cost: |
| **Campground Notes:** | ❑ Full Hookups   ❑ 50-amp   ❑ Showers   ❑ Laundry   ❑ RV Dump   ❑ Wi-Fi   ❑ Camp Store | | | | | |
| | *Noise:* ❑ Quiet ❑ Some ❑ Noisy ◆ *Overall:* ❑ Poor ❑ Fair ❑ Good ❑ Excellent | | | | | |
| **Overnight Parking Notes:** | | | | | | |
| | *Noise:* ❑ Quiet ❑ Some ❑ Noisy ◆ *Overall:* ❑ Poor ❑ Fair ❑ Good ❑ Excellent | | | | | |
| **Dinner:** | | | | | | |
| **People Met Today:** | | | | | | |

# Miscellaneous Notes

| Other Notes About Today's Journey: | |
|---|---|
| *Suggestions:* | |
| ✦ *Things to see and do next time* | |
| ✦ *Weather conditions* | |
| ✦ *Anything else you want to remember!* | |

# The Journey

| Departure: | Date: | Time: | Holiday? ❑ Yes ❑ No |
|---|---|---|---|
| **Departed From**: | | | |
| **Destination**: | | | |
| **Arrival**: | Time: | Hours Traveled: | |
| **Mileage**: | Start: | End: | Total: |
| **Planned Travel Routes**: | | | |

# Along the Way

**My Notes Along the Way**:

*Suggestions:*

✧ *Attractions*
✧ *Cities and towns traveled through*
✧ *Eats and treats*
✧ *Points of interest*
✧ *Routes followed*
✧ *Routes to avoid*
✧ *Scenic views*
✧ *Shopping*
✧ *Wildlife seen*
✧ *Anything else you experience along the way!*

# Day's End

| Stayed Overnight: | ❑ Campground    ❑ Cracker Barrel    ❑ Walmart    ❑ Other: |
|---|---|
| **Campground Name:** | Site #:      Cost: |
| **Campground Notes:** | ❑ Full Hookups   ❑ 50-amp   ❑ Showers   ❑ Laundry   ❑ RV Dump   ❑ Wi-Fi   ❑ Camp Store <br><br><br><br><br><br> *Noise:* ❑ Quiet ❑ Some ❑ Noisy • *Overall:* ❑ Poor ❑ Fair ❑ Good ❑ Excellent |
| **Overnight Parking Notes:** | <br><br> *Noise:* ❑ Quiet ❑ Some ❑ Noisy • *Overall:* ❑ Poor ❑ Fair ❑ Good ❑ Excellent |
| **Dinner:** | |
| **People Met Today:** | |

# Miscellaneous Notes

| **Other Notes About Today's Journey:** <br><br> *Suggestions:* <br><br> ✧ *Things to see and do next time* <br> ✧ *Weather conditions* <br> ✧ *Anything else you want to remember!* | |
|---|---|

# The Journey

| Departure: | Date: | | Time: | Holiday? ❑ Yes ❑ No |
|---|---|---|---|---|
| **Departed From:** | | | | |
| **Destination:** | | | | |
| **Arrival:** | Time: | | Hours Traveled: | |
| **Mileage:** | Start: | End: | Total: | |
| **Planned Travel Routes:** | | | | |

# Along the Way

**My Notes Along the Way:**

*Suggestions:*

✧   *Attractions*

✧   *Cities and towns traveled through*

✧   *Eats and treats*

✧   *Points of interest*

✧   *Routes followed*

✧   *Routes to avoid*

✧   *Scenic views*

✧   *Shopping*

✧   *Wildlife seen*

✧   *Anything else you experience along the way!*

# Day's End

| Stayed Overnight: | ❑ Campground   ❑ Cracker Barrel   ❑ Walmart   ❑ Other: |
|---|---|
| **Campground Name:** | Site #:          Cost: |
| **Campground Notes:** | ❑ Full Hookups   ❑ 50-amp   ❑ Showers   ❑ Laundry   ❑ RV Dump   ❑ Wi-Fi   ❑ Camp Store<br><br><br><br><br><br>*Noise:* ❑ Quiet ❑ Some ❑ Noisy  ◆ *Overall:* ❑ Poor ❑ Fair ❑ Good ❑ Excellent |
| **Overnight Parking Notes:** | <br><br>*Noise:* ❑ Quiet ❑ Some ❑ Noisy  ◆ *Overall:* ❑ Poor ❑ Fair ❑ Good ❑ Excellent |
| **Dinner:** | |
| **People Met Today:** | |

# Miscellaneous Notes

| **Other Notes About Today's Journey:**<br><br>*Suggestions:*<br><br>✦ *Things to see and do next time*<br>✦ *Weather conditions*<br>✦ *Anything else you want to remember!* | |
|---|---|

# The Journey

| Departure: | Date: | | Time: | Holiday? ❏ Yes ❏ No |
|---|---|---|---|---|
| **Departed From**: | | | | |
| **Destination**: | | | | |
| **Arrival**: | Time: | | Hours Traveled: | |
| **Mileage**: | Start: | End: | Total: | |
| **Planned Travel Routes**: | | | | |

# Along the Way

**My Notes Along the Way**:

*Suggestions:*

◇  *Attractions*

◇  *Cities and towns traveled through*

◇  *Eats and treats*

◇  *Points of interest*

◇  *Routes followed*

◇  *Routes to avoid*

◇  *Scenic views*

◇  *Shopping*

◇  *Wildlife seen*

◇  *Anything else you experience along the way!*

# Day's End

| Stayed Overnight: | ❑ Campground    ❑ Cracker Barrel    ❑ Walmart    ❑ Other: |
|---|---|
| **Campground Name:** | Site #:                    Cost: |
| **Campground Notes:** | ❑ Full Hookups   ❑ 50-amp   ❑ Showers   ❑ Laundry   ❑ RV Dump   ❑ Wi-Fi   ❑ Camp Store <br><br><br><br><br><br><br> *Noise:* ❑ Quiet ❑ Some ❑ Noisy ◆ *Overall:* ❑ Poor ❑ Fair ❑ Good ❑ Excellent |
| **Overnight Parking Notes:** | <br><br><br> *Noise:* ❑ Quiet ❑ Some ❑ Noisy ◆ *Overall:* ❑ Poor ❑ Fair ❑ Good ❑ Excellent |
| **Dinner:** | |
| **People Met Today:** | |

# Miscellaneous Notes

| Other Notes About Today's Journey: <br><br> *Suggestions:* <br><br> ✧ *Things to see and do next time* <br> ✧ *Weather conditions* <br> ✧ *Anything else you want to remember!* | |
|---|---|

# The Journey

| Departure: | Date: | | Time: | | Holiday? ☐ Yes ☐ No |
|---|---|---|---|---|---|
| **Departed From:** | | | | | |
| **Destination:** | | | | | |
| **Arrival:** | Time: | | Hours Traveled: | | |
| **Mileage:** | Start: | End: | | Total: | |
| **Planned Travel Routes:** | | | | | |

# Along the Way

**My Notes Along the Way:**

*Suggestions:*

- ✧ *Attractions*
- ✧ *Cities and towns traveled through*
- ✧ *Eats and treats*
- ✧ *Points of interest*
- ✧ *Routes followed*
- ✧ *Routes to avoid*
- ✧ *Scenic views*
- ✧ *Shopping*
- ✧ *Wildlife seen*
- ✧ *Anything else you experience along the way!*

# Day's End

| Stayed Overnight: | ❑ Campground  ❑ Cracker Barrel  ❑ Walmart  ❑ Other: |
|---|---|
| Campground Name: | Site #:          Cost: |
| Campground Notes: | ❑ Full Hookups  ❑ 50-amp  ❑ Showers  ❑ Laundry  ❑ RV Dump  ❑ Wi-Fi  ❑ Camp Store<br><br><br><br><br><br>*Noise:* ❑ Quiet  ❑ Some  ❑ Noisy  •  *Overall:* ❑ Poor  ❑ Fair  ❑ Good  ❑ Excellent |
| Overnight Parking Notes: | <br><br>*Noise:* ❑ Quiet  ❑ Some  ❑ Noisy  •  *Overall:* ❑ Poor  ❑ Fair  ❑ Good  ❑ Excellent |
| Dinner: | |
| People Met Today: | |

# Miscellaneous Notes

| Other Notes About Today's Journey:<br><br>*Suggestions:*<br><br>✧ *Things to see and do next time*<br>✧ *Weather conditions*<br>✧ *Anything else you want to remember!* | |
|---|---|

# The Journey

| Departure: | Date: | | Time: | | Holiday? ❑ Yes ❑ No |
|---|---|---|---|---|---|
| **Departed From**: | | | | | |
| **Destination**: | | | | | |
| **Arrival**: | Time: | | Hours Traveled: | | |
| **Mileage**: | Start: | End: | | Total: | |
| **Planned Travel Routes**: | | | | | |

# Along the Way

| **My Notes Along the Way**: | |
|---|---|
| *Suggestions:* | |
| ✧ *Attractions* | |
| ✧ *Cities and towns traveled through* | |
| ✧ *Eats and treats* | |
| ✧ *Points of interest* | |
| ✧ *Routes followed* | |
| ✧ *Routes to avoid* | |
| ✧ *Scenic views* | |
| ✧ *Shopping* | |
| ✧ *Wildlife seen* | |
| ✧ *Anything else you experience along the way!* | |

# Day's End

| Stayed Overnight: | ❑ Campground   ❑ Cracker Barrel   ❑ Walmart   ❑ Other: |
|---|---|
| **Campground Name:** | Site #:          Cost: |
| **Campground Notes:** | ❑ Full Hookups   ❑ 50-amp   ❑ Showers   ❑ Laundry   ❑ RV Dump   ❑ Wi-Fi   ❑ Camp Store <br><br><br><br><br><br><br> *Noise:* ❑ Quiet ❑ Some ❑ Noisy ◆ *Overall:* ❑ Poor ❑ Fair ❑ Good ❑ Excellent |
| **Overnight Parking Notes:** | <br><br><br> *Noise:* ❑ Quiet ❑ Some ❑ Noisy ◆ *Overall:* ❑ Poor ❑ Fair ❑ Good ❑ Excellent |
| **Dinner:** | |
| **People Met Today:** | |

# Miscellaneous Notes

| Other Notes About Today's Journey: <br><br> *Suggestions:* <br><br> ✧ *Things to see and do next time* <br> ✧ *Weather conditions* <br> ✧ *Anything else you want to remember!* | |
|---|---|

# The Journey

| Departure: | Date: | | Time: | | Holiday? ❑ Yes ❑ No |
|---|---|---|---|---|---|
| **Departed From**: | | | | | |
| **Destination**: | | | | | |
| **Arrival**: | Time: | | Hours Traveled: | | |
| **Mileage**: | Start: | End: | | Total: | |
| **Planned Travel Routes**: | | | | | |

# Along the Way

| My Notes Along the Way: | |
|---|---|
| *Suggestions:* | |
| ✧ *Attractions* | |
| ✧ *Cities and towns traveled through* | |
| ✧ *Eats and treats* | |
| ✧ *Points of interest* | |
| ✧ *Routes followed* | |
| ✧ *Routes to avoid* | |
| ✧ *Scenic views* | |
| ✧ *Shopping* | |
| ✧ *Wildlife seen* | |
| ✧ *Anything else you experience along the way!* | |

# Day's End

| | |
|---|---|
| **Stayed Overnight:** | ❑ Campground    ❑ Cracker Barrel    ❑ Walmart    ❑ Other: |
| **Campground Name:** | Site #:          Cost: |
| **Campground Notes:** | ❑ Full Hookups   ❑ 50-amp   ❑ Showers   ❑ Laundry   ❑ RV Dump   ❑ Wi-Fi   ❑ Camp Store <br><br><br><br><br><br><br> *Noise:* ❑ Quiet ❑ Some ❑ Noisy ⬥ *Overall:* ❑ Poor ❑ Fair ❑ Good ❑ Excellent |
| **Overnight Parking Notes:** | <br><br> *Noise:* ❑ Quiet ❑ Some ❑ Noisy ⬥ *Overall:* ❑ Poor ❑ Fair ❑ Good ❑ Excellent |
| **Dinner:** | |
| **People Met Today:** | |

# Miscellaneous Notes

| | |
|---|---|
| **Other Notes About Today's Journey:** <br><br> *Suggestions:* <br><br> ✧ *Things to see and do next time* <br> ✧ *Weather conditions* <br> ✧ *Anything else you want to remember!* | |

# The Journey

| Departure: | Date: | Time: | Holiday? ❑ Yes ❑ No |
|---|---|---|---|
| **Departed From:** | | | |
| **Destination:** | | | |
| **Arrival:** | Time: | Hours Traveled: | |
| **Mileage:** | Start: | End: | Total: |
| **Planned Travel Routes:** | | | |

# Along the Way

**My Notes Along the Way:**

*Suggestions:*

✧ *Attractions*

✧ *Cities and towns traveled through*

✧ *Eats and treats*

✧ *Points of interest*

✧ *Routes followed*

✧ *Routes to avoid*

✧ *Scenic views*

✧ *Shopping*

✧ *Wildlife seen*

✧ *Anything else you experience along the way!*

# Day's End

| Stayed Overnight: | ❑ Campground  ❑ Cracker Barrel  ❑ Walmart  ❑ Other: |
|---|---|
| **Campground Name:** | Site #:          Cost: |
| **Campground Notes:** | ❑ Full Hookups  ❑ 50-amp  ❑ Showers  ❑ Laundry  ❑ RV Dump  ❑ Wi-Fi  ❑ Camp Store<br><br><br><br><br><br><br>*Noise:* ❑ Quiet ❑ Some ❑ Noisy ◆ *Overall:* ❑ Poor ❑ Fair ❑ Good ❑ Excellent |
| **Overnight Parking Notes:** | <br><br>*Noise:* ❑ Quiet ❑ Some ❑ Noisy ◆ *Overall:* ❑ Poor ❑ Fair ❑ Good ❑ Excellent |
| **Dinner:** | |
| **People Met Today:** | |

# Miscellaneous Notes

| Other Notes About Today's Journey:<br><br>*Suggestions:*<br><br>✧ *Things to see and do next time*<br>✧ *Weather conditions*<br>✧ *Anything else you want to remember!* | |
|---|---|

# The Journey

| Departure: | Date: | Time: | Holiday? ❏ Yes ❏ No |
|---|---|---|---|
| **Departed From**: | | | |
| **Destination**: | | | |
| **Arrival**: | Time: | Hours Traveled: | |
| **Mileage**: | Start: | End: | Total: |
| **Planned Travel Routes**: | | | |

# Along the Way

| **My Notes Along the Way**: | |
|---|---|
| *Suggestions:* | |
| ✧ *Attractions* | |
| ✧ *Cities and towns traveled through* | |
| ✧ *Eats and treats* | |
| ✧ *Points of interest* | |
| ✧ *Routes followed* | |
| ✧ *Routes to avoid* | |
| ✧ *Scenic views* | |
| ✧ *Shopping* | |
| ✧ *Wildlife seen* | |
| ✧ *Anything else you experience along the way!* | |

# Day's End

| Stayed Overnight: | ❑ Campground   ❑ Cracker Barrel   ❑ Walmart   ❑ Other: |
|---|---|
| **Campground Name:** | Site #:                Cost: |
| **Campground Notes:** | ❑ Full Hookups   ❑ 50-amp   ❑ Showers   ❑ Laundry   ❑ RV Dump   ❑ Wi-Fi   ❑ Camp Store

*Noise:* ❑ Quiet ❑ Some ❑ Noisy ♦ *Overall:* ❑ Poor ❑ Fair ❑ Good ❑ Excellent |
| **Overnight Parking Notes:** | *Noise:* ❑ Quiet ❑ Some ❑ Noisy ♦ *Overall:* ❑ Poor ❑ Fair ❑ Good ❑ Excellent |
| **Dinner:** | |
| **People Met Today:** | |

# Miscellaneous Notes

| **Other Notes About Today's Journey:**

*Suggestions:*

 ✧ *Things to see and do next time*

 ✧ *Weather conditions*

 ✧ *Anything else you want to remember!* | |
|---|---|

# The Journey

| Departure: | Date: | Time: | Holiday? ☐ Yes ☐ No |
|---|---|---|---|
| **Departed From:** | | | |
| **Destination:** | | | |
| **Arrival:** | Time: | Hours Traveled: | |
| **Mileage:** | Start: | End: | Total: |
| **Planned Travel Routes:** | | | |

# Along the Way

| My Notes Along the Way: | |
|---|---|
| *Suggestions:* | |
| ✧ *Attractions* | |
| ✧ *Cities and towns traveled through* | |
| ✧ *Eats and treats* | |
| ✧ *Points of interest* | |
| ✧ *Routes followed* | |
| ✧ *Routes to avoid* | |
| ✧ *Scenic views* | |
| ✧ *Shopping* | |
| ✧ *Wildlife seen* | |
| ✧ *Anything else you experience along the way!* | |

# Day's End

| Stayed Overnight: | ☐ Campground    ☐ Cracker Barrel    ☐ Walmart    ☐ Other: |
|---|---|
| **Campground Name:** | Site #:          Cost: |
| **Campground Notes:** | ☐ Full Hookups    ☐ 50-amp    ☐ Showers    ☐ Laundry    ☐ RV Dump    ☐ Wi-Fi    ☐ Camp Store<br><br><br><br><br><br>*Noise:* ☐ Quiet ☐ Some ☐ Noisy  •  *Overall:* ☐ Poor ☐ Fair ☐ Good ☐ Excellent |
| **Overnight Parking Notes:** | <br><br><br>*Noise:* ☐ Quiet ☐ Some ☐ Noisy  •  *Overall:* ☐ Poor ☐ Fair ☐ Good ☐ Excellent |
| **Dinner:** | |
| **People Met Today:** | |

# Miscellaneous Notes

| Other Notes About Today's Journey:<br><br>*Suggestions:*<br><br>✧  *Things to see and do next time*<br><br>✧  *Weather conditions*<br><br>✧  *Anything else you want to remember!* | |
|---|---|

# The Journey

| Departure: | Date: | Time: | Holiday? ❑ Yes ❑ No |
|---|---|---|---|
| **Departed From:** | | | |
| **Destination:** | | | |
| **Arrival:** | Time: | Hours Traveled: | |
| **Mileage:** | Start: | End: | Total: |
| **Planned Travel Routes:** | | | |

# Along the Way

| My Notes Along the Way: | |
|---|---|
| *Suggestions:* | |
| ✧ *Attractions* | |
| ✧ *Cities and towns traveled through* | |
| ✧ *Eats and treats* | |
| ✧ *Points of interest* | |
| ✧ *Routes followed* | |
| ✧ *Routes to avoid* | |
| ✧ *Scenic views* | |
| ✧ *Shopping* | |
| ✧ *Wildlife seen* | |
| ✧ *Anything else you experience along the way!* | |

# Day's End

| Stayed Overnight: | ❑ Campground   ❑ Cracker Barrel   ❑ Walmart   ❑ Other: |
|---|---|
| **Campground Name:** | Site #:          Cost: |
| **Campground Notes:** | ❑ Full Hookups   ❑ 50-amp   ❑ Showers   ❑ Laundry   ❑ RV Dump   ❑ Wi-Fi   ❑ Camp Store<br><br><br><br><br><br>*Noise:* ❑ Quiet ❑ Some ❑ Noisy  •  *Overall:* ❑ Poor ❑ Fair ❑ Good ❑ Excellent |
| **Overnight Parking Notes:** | <br><br><br>*Noise:* ❑ Quiet ❑ Some ❑ Noisy  •  *Overall:* ❑ Poor ❑ Fair ❑ Good ❑ Excellent |
| **Dinner:** | |
| **People Met Today:** | |

# Miscellaneous Notes

| Other Notes About Today's Journey: <br><br>*Suggestions:* <br><br>✧  *Things to see and do next time* <br>✧  *Weather conditions* <br>✧  *Anything else you want to remember!* | |
|---|---|

# The Journey

| Departure: | Date: | | Time: | | Holiday? ❑ Yes ❑ No |
|---|---|---|---|---|---|
| **Departed From:** | | | | | |
| **Destination:** | | | | | |
| **Arrival:** | Time: | | Hours Traveled: | | |
| **Mileage:** | Start: | End: | | Total: | |
| **Planned Travel Routes:** | | | | | |

# Along the Way

| My Notes Along the Way: | |
|---|---|
| *Suggestions:* | |
| ✧ *Attractions* | |
| ✧ *Cities and towns traveled through* | |
| ✧ *Eats and treats* | |
| ✧ *Points of interest* | |
| ✧ *Routes followed* | |
| ✧ *Routes to avoid* | |
| ✧ *Scenic views* | |
| ✧ *Shopping* | |
| ✧ *Wildlife seen* | |
| ✧ *Anything else you experience along the way!* | |

# Day's End

| Stayed Overnight: | ❑ Campground ❑ Cracker Barrel ❑ Walmart ❑ Other: |
|---|---|
| **Campground Name:** | Site #:      Cost: |
| **Campground Notes:** | ❑ Full Hookups ❑ 50-amp ❑ Showers ❑ Laundry ❑ RV Dump ❑ Wi-Fi ❑ Camp Store<br><br><br><br><br><br>*Noise:* ❑ Quiet ❑ Some ❑ Noisy • *Overall:* ❑ Poor ❑ Fair ❑ Good ❑ Excellent |
| **Overnight Parking Notes:** | <br><br>*Noise:* ❑ Quiet ❑ Some ❑ Noisy • *Overall:* ❑ Poor ❑ Fair ❑ Good ❑ Excellent |
| **Dinner:** | |
| **People Met Today:** | |

# Miscellaneous Notes

| **Other Notes About Today's Journey:**<br><br>*Suggestions:*<br><br>✧ *Things to see and do next time*<br>✧ *Weather conditions*<br>✧ *Anything else you want to remember!* | |
|---|---|

# The Journey

| Departure: | Date: | | Time: | | Holiday? ❑ Yes ❑ No |
|---|---|---|---|---|---|
| **Departed From:** | | | | | |
| **Destination:** | | | | | |
| **Arrival:** | Time: | | Hours Traveled: | | |
| **Mileage:** | Start: | End: | | Total: | |
| **Planned Travel Routes:** | | | | | |

# Along the Way

**My Notes Along the Way:**

*Suggestions:*

- ✧ *Attractions*
- ✧ *Cities and towns traveled through*
- ✧ *Eats and treats*
- ✧ *Points of interest*
- ✧ *Routes followed*
- ✧ *Routes to avoid*
- ✧ *Scenic views*
- ✧ *Shopping*
- ✧ *Wildlife seen*
- ✧ *Anything else you experience along the way!*

# Day's End

| | |
|---|---|
| **Stayed Overnight:** | ❑ Campground    ❑ Cracker Barrel    ❑ Walmart    ❑ Other: |
| **Campground Name:** | Site #:          Cost: |
| **Campground Notes:** | ❑ Full Hookups    ❑ 50-amp    ❑ Showers    ❑ Laundry    ❑ RV Dump    ❑ Wi-Fi    ❑ Camp Store<br><br><br><br><br><br><br>*Noise:* ❑ Quiet ❑ Some ❑ Noisy • *Overall:* ❑ Poor ❑ Fair ❑ Good ❑ Excellent |
| **Overnight Parking Notes:** | <br><br><br><br>*Noise:* ❑ Quiet ❑ Some ❑ Noisy • *Overall:* ❑ Poor ❑ Fair ❑ Good ❑ Excellent |
| **Dinner:** | |
| **People Met Today:** | |

# Miscellaneous Notes

| | |
|---|---|
| **Other Notes About Today's Journey:**<br><br>*Suggestions:*<br><br>✧ *Things to see and do next time*<br>✧ *Weather conditions*<br>✧ *Anything else you want to remember!* | |

# The Journey

| Departure: | Date: | | Time: | | Holiday? ❑ Yes ❑ No |
|---|---|---|---|---|---|
| **Departed From:** | | | | | |
| **Destination:** | | | | | |
| **Arrival:** | Time: | | Hours Traveled: | | |
| **Mileage:** | Start: | End: | | Total: | |
| **Planned Travel Routes:** | | | | | |

# Along the Way

**My Notes Along the Way:**

*Suggestions:*

- ✦  *Attractions*
- ✦  *Cities and towns traveled through*
- ✦  *Eats and treats*
- ✦  *Points of interest*
- ✦  *Routes followed*
- ✦  *Routes to avoid*
- ✦  *Scenic views*
- ✦  *Shopping*
- ✦  *Wildlife seen*
- ✦  *Anything else you experience along the way!*

# Day's End

| Stayed Overnight: | ❑ Campground ❑ Cracker Barrel ❑ Walmart ❑ Other: |
|---|---|
| Campground Name: | Site #: Cost: |
| Campground Notes: | ❑ Full Hookups ❑ 50-amp ❑ Showers ❑ Laundry ❑ RV Dump ❑ Wi-Fi ❑ Camp Store <br><br><br><br><br><br>*Noise:* ❑ Quiet ❑ Some ❑ Noisy • *Overall:* ❑ Poor ❑ Fair ❑ Good ❑ Excellent |
| Overnight Parking Notes: | <br><br><br>*Noise:* ❑ Quiet ❑ Some ❑ Noisy • *Overall:* ❑ Poor ❑ Fair ❑ Good ❑ Excellent |
| Dinner: | |
| People Met Today: | |

# Miscellaneous Notes

| Other Notes About Today's Journey: <br><br>*Suggestions:* <br><br>✧ *Things to see and do next time* <br>✧ *Weather conditions* <br>✧ *Anything else you want to remember!* | |
|---|---|

# The Journey

| Departure: | Date: | Time: | Holiday? ☐ Yes ☐ No |
|---|---|---|---|
| **Departed From**: | | | |
| **Destination**: | | | |
| **Arrival**: | Time: | Hours Traveled: | |
| **Mileage**: | Start: | End: | Total: |
| **Planned Travel Routes**: | | | |

# Along the Way

**My Notes Along the Way**:

*Suggestions:*

✧ *Attractions*

✧ *Cities and towns traveled through*

✧ *Eats and treats*

✧ *Points of interest*

✧ *Routes followed*

✧ *Routes to avoid*

✧ *Scenic views*

✧ *Shopping*

✧ *Wildlife seen*

✧ *Anything else you experience along the way!*

# Day's End

| Stayed Overnight: | ❑ Campground ❑ Cracker Barrel ❑ Walmart ❑ Other: |
|---|---|
| Campground Name: | Site #:          Cost: |
| Campground Notes: | ❑ Full Hookups  ❑ 50-amp  ❑ Showers  ❑ Laundry  ❑ RV Dump  ❑ Wi-Fi  ❑ Camp Store |
| | *Noise:* ❑ Quiet ❑ Some ❑ Noisy ◆ *Overall:* ❑ Poor ❑ Fair ❑ Good ❑ Excellent |
| Overnight Parking Notes: | |
| | *Noise:* ❑ Quiet ❑ Some ❑ Noisy ◆ *Overall:* ❑ Poor ❑ Fair ❑ Good ❑ Excellent |
| Dinner: | |
| People Met Today: | |

# Miscellaneous Notes

| Other Notes About Today's Journey:  *Suggestions:*  ✧ *Things to see and do next time*  ✧ *Weather conditions*  ✧ *Anything else you want to remember!* | |
|---|---|

# The Journey

| Departure: | Date: | | Time: | | Holiday? ☐ Yes ☐ No |
|---|---|---|---|---|---|
| **Departed From:** | | | | | |
| **Destination:** | | | | | |
| **Arrival:** | Time: | | Hours Traveled: | | |
| **Mileage:** | Start: | End: | | Total: | |
| **Planned Travel Routes:** | | | | | |

# Along the Way

**My Notes Along the Way:**

*Suggestions:*

- ✧ *Attractions*
- ✧ *Cities and towns traveled through*
- ✧ *Eats and treats*
- ✧ *Points of interest*
- ✧ *Routes followed*
- ✧ *Routes to avoid*
- ✧ *Scenic views*
- ✧ *Shopping*
- ✧ *Wildlife seen*
- ✧ *Anything else you experience along the way!*

# Day's End

| Stayed Overnight: | ❑ Campground  ❑ Cracker Barrel  ❑ Walmart  ❑ Other: |
|---|---|
| **Campground Name:** | Site #:          Cost: |
| **Campground Notes:** | ❑ Full Hookups  ❑ 50-amp  ❑ Showers  ❑ Laundry  ❑ RV Dump  ❑ Wi-Fi  ❑ Camp Store |
| | |
| | *Noise:* ❑ Quiet ❑ Some ❑ Noisy  ◆  *Overall:* ❑ Poor ❑ Fair ❑ Good ❑ Excellent |
| **Overnight Parking Notes:** | |
| | *Noise:* ❑ Quiet ❑ Some ❑ Noisy  ◆  *Overall:* ❑ Poor ❑ Fair ❑ Good ❑ Excellent |
| **Dinner:** | |
| **People Met Today:** | |

# Miscellaneous Notes

| **Other Notes About Today's Journey:** *Suggestions:* ✧ *Things to see and do next time* ✧ *Weather conditions* ✧ *Anything else you want to remember!* | |
|---|---|

# The Journey

| Departure: | Date: | Time: | Holiday?  ☐ Yes ☐ No |
|---|---|---|---|
| **Departed From**: | | | |
| **Destination**: | | | |
| **Arrival**: | Time: | Hours Traveled: | |
| **Mileage**: | Start: | End: | Total: |
| **Planned Travel Routes**: | | | |

# Along the Way

**My Notes Along the Way:**

*Suggestions:*

✦ *Attractions*

✦ *Cities and towns traveled through*

✦ *Eats and treats*

✦ *Points of interest*

✦ *Routes followed*

✦ *Routes to avoid*

✦ *Scenic views*

✦ *Shopping*

✦ *Wildlife seen*

✦ *Anything else you experience along the way!*

# Day's End

| Stayed Overnight: | ❑ Campground    ❑ Cracker Barrel    ❑ Walmart    ❑ Other: |
|---|---|
| Campground Name: | Site #:                    Cost: |
| Campground Notes: | ❑ Full Hookups    ❑ 50-amp    ❑ Showers    ❑ Laundry    ❑ RV Dump    ❑ Wi-Fi    ❑ Camp Store |
| | |
| | *Noise:* ❑ Quiet ❑ Some ❑ Noisy • *Overall:* ❑ Poor ❑ Fair ❑ Good ❑ Excellent |
| Overnight Parking Notes: | |
| | *Noise:* ❑ Quiet ❑ Some ❑ Noisy • *Overall:* ❑ Poor ❑ Fair ❑ Good ❑ Excellent |
| Dinner: | |
| People Met Today: | |

# Miscellaneous Notes

| Other Notes About Today's Journey:

*Suggestions:*

✧ *Things to see and do next time*
✧ *Weather conditions*
✧ *Anything else you want to remember!* | |
|---|---|

# The Journey

| Departure: | Date: | | Time: | Holiday? ☐ Yes ☐ No |
|---|---|---|---|---|
| **Departed From:** | | | | |
| **Destination:** | | | | |
| **Arrival:** | Time: | | Hours Traveled: | |
| **Mileage:** | Start: | End: | Total: | |
| **Planned Travel Routes:** | | | | |

# Along the Way

**My Notes Along the Way:**

*Suggestions:*

⬥ *Attractions*

⬥ *Cities and towns traveled through*

⬥ *Eats and treats*

⬥ *Points of interest*

⬥ *Routes followed*

⬥ *Routes to avoid*

⬥ *Scenic views*

⬥ *Shopping*

⬥ *Wildlife seen*

⬥ *Anything else you experience along the way!*

# Day's End

| Stayed Overnight: | ❑ Campground ❑ Cracker Barrel ❑ Walmart ❑ Other: |
|---|---|
| **Campground Name:** | Site #: Cost: |
| **Campground Notes:** | ❑ Full Hookups ❑ 50-amp ❑ Showers ❑ Laundry ❑ RV Dump ❑ Wi-Fi ❑ Camp Store <br><br><br><br><br><br> *Noise:* ❑ Quiet ❑ Some ❑ Noisy • *Overall:* ❑ Poor ❑ Fair ❑ Good ❑ Excellent |
| **Overnight Parking Notes:** | <br><br> *Noise:* ❑ Quiet ❑ Some ❑ Noisy • *Overall:* ❑ Poor ❑ Fair ❑ Good ❑ Excellent |
| **Dinner:** | |
| **People Met Today:** | |

# Miscellaneous Notes

| **Other Notes About Today's Journey:** *Suggestions:* ✧ *Things to see and do next time* ✧ *Weather conditions* ✧ *Anything else you want to remember!* | |
|---|---|

# The Journey

| Departure: | Date: | Time: | Holiday? ☐ Yes ☐ No |
|---|---|---|---|
| **Departed From**: | | | |
| **Destination**: | | | |
| **Arrival**: | Time: | Hours Traveled: | |
| **Mileage**: | Start: | End: | Total: |
| **Planned Travel Routes**: | | | |

# Along the Way

**My Notes Along the Way**:

*Suggestions:*

◇ *Attractions*

◇ *Cities and towns traveled through*

◇ *Eats and treats*

◇ *Points of interest*

◇ *Routes followed*

◇ *Routes to avoid*

◇ *Scenic views*

◇ *Shopping*

◇ *Wildlife seen*

◇ *Anything else you experience along the way!*

# Day's End

| Stayed Overnight: | ❏ Campground ❏ Cracker Barrel ❏ Walmart ❏ Other: |
|---|---|
| **Campground Name:** | Site #:      Cost: |
| **Campground Notes:** | ❏ Full Hookups ❏ 50-amp ❏ Showers ❏ Laundry ❏ RV Dump ❏ Wi-Fi ❏ Camp Store<br><br><br><br><br><br>*Noise:* ❏ Quiet ❏ Some ❏ Noisy ◆ *Overall:* ❏ Poor ❏ Fair ❏ Good ❏ Excellent |
| **Overnight Parking Notes:** | <br><br><br>*Noise:* ❏ Quiet ❏ Some ❏ Noisy ◆ *Overall:* ❏ Poor ❏ Fair ❏ Good ❏ Excellent |
| **Dinner:** | |
| **People Met Today:** | |

# Miscellaneous Notes

| **Other Notes About Today's Journey:**<br><br>*Suggestions:*<br><br>✦ *Things to see and do next time*<br>✦ *Weather conditions*<br>✦ *Anything else you want to remember!* | |
|---|---|

# The Journey

| Departure: | Date: | | Time: | | Holiday?  ☐ Yes  ☐ No |
|---|---|---|---|---|---|
| **Departed From:** | | | | | |
| **Destination:** | | | | | |
| **Arrival:** | Time: | | Hours Traveled: | | |
| **Mileage:** | Start: | End: | | Total: | |
| **Planned Travel Routes:** | | | | | |

# Along the Way

**My Notes Along the Way:**

*Suggestions:*

✧  *Attractions*

✧  *Cities and towns traveled through*

✧  *Eats and treats*

✧  *Points of interest*

✧  *Routes followed*

✧  *Routes to avoid*

✧  *Scenic views*

✧  *Shopping*

✧  *Wildlife seen*

✧  *Anything else you experience along the way!*

# Day's End

| | |
|---|---|
| **Stayed Overnight:** | ❑ Campground   ❑ Cracker Barrel   ❑ Walmart   ❑ Other: |
| **Campground Name:** | Site #:        Cost: |
| **Campground Notes:** | ❑ Full Hookups   ❑ 50-amp   ❑ Showers   ❑ Laundry   ❑ RV Dump   ❑ Wi-Fi   ❑ Camp Store |
| | *Noise:* ❑ Quiet ❑ Some ❑ Noisy ◆ *Overall:* ❑ Poor ❑ Fair ❑ Good ❑ Excellent |
| **Overnight Parking Notes:** | |
| | *Noise:* ❑ Quiet ❑ Some ❑ Noisy ◆ *Overall:* ❑ Poor ❑ Fair ❑ Good ❑ Excellent |
| **Dinner:** | |
| **People Met Today:** | |

# Miscellaneous Notes

| | |
|---|---|
| **Other Notes About Today's Journey:**  *Suggestions:*  ✧ *Things to see and do next time*  ✧ *Weather conditions*  ✧ *Anything else you want to remember!* | |

# The Journey

| Departure: | Date: | Time: | Holiday?  ☐ Yes  ☐ No |
|---|---|---|---|
| **Departed From:** | | | |
| **Destination:** | | | |
| **Arrival:** | Time: | Hours Traveled: | |
| **Mileage:** | Start: | End: | Total: |
| **Planned Travel Routes:** | | | |

# Along the Way

**My Notes Along the Way:**

*Suggestions:*

- ✧ *Attractions*
- ✧ *Cities and towns traveled through*
- ✧ *Eats and treats*
- ✧ *Points of interest*
- ✧ *Routes followed*
- ✧ *Routes to avoid*
- ✧ *Scenic views*
- ✧ *Shopping*
- ✧ *Wildlife seen*
- ✧ *Anything else you experience along the way!*

# Day's End

| Stayed Overnight: | ❑ Campground ❑ Cracker Barrel ❑ Walmart ❑ Other: |
|---|---|
| **Campground Name:** | Site #: Cost: |
| **Campground Notes:** | ❑ Full Hookups ❑ 50-amp ❑ Showers ❑ Laundry ❑ RV Dump ❑ Wi-Fi ❑ Camp Store <br><br><br><br><br> *Noise:* ❑ Quiet ❑ Some ❑ Noisy • *Overall:* ❑ Poor ❑ Fair ❑ Good ❑ Excellent |
| **Overnight Parking Notes:** | <br><br> *Noise:* ❑ Quiet ❑ Some ❑ Noisy • *Overall:* ❑ Poor ❑ Fair ❑ Good ❑ Excellent |
| **Dinner:** | |
| **People Met Today:** | |

# Miscellaneous Notes

| **Other Notes About Today's Journey:** <br><br> *Suggestions:* <br><br> ✧ *Things to see and do next time* <br> ✧ *Weather conditions* <br> ✧ *Anything else you want to remember!* | |
|---|---|

# The Journey

| Departure: | Date: | | Time: | Holiday? ☐ Yes ☐ No |
|---|---|---|---|---|
| **Departed From:** | | | | |
| **Destination:** | | | | |
| **Arrival:** | Time: | | Hours Traveled: | |
| **Mileage:** | Start: | End: | Total: | |
| **Planned Travel Routes:** | | | | |

# Along the Way

**My Notes Along the Way:**

*Suggestions:*

- ✧ *Attractions*
- ✧ *Cities and towns traveled through*
- ✧ *Eats and treats*
- ✧ *Points of interest*
- ✧ *Routes followed*
- ✧ *Routes to avoid*
- ✧ *Scenic views*
- ✧ *Shopping*
- ✧ *Wildlife seen*
- ✧ *Anything else you experience along the way!*

# Day's End

| Stayed Overnight: | ❑ Campground    ❑ Cracker Barrel    ❑ Walmart    ❑ Other: |
|---|---|
| **Campground Name:** | Site #:      Cost: |
| **Campground Notes:** | ❑ Full Hookups   ❑ 50-amp   ❑ Showers   ❑ Laundry   ❑ RV Dump   ❑ Wi-Fi   ❑ Camp Store <br><br><br><br><br><br><br> *Noise:* ❑ Quiet ❑ Some ❑ Noisy ◆ *Overall:* ❑ Poor ❑ Fair ❑ Good ❑ Excellent |
| **Overnight Parking Notes:** | <br><br><br> *Noise:* ❑ Quiet ❑ Some ❑ Noisy ◆ *Overall:* ❑ Poor ❑ Fair ❑ Good ❑ Excellent |
| **Dinner:** | |
| **People Met Today:** | |

# Miscellaneous Notes

| **Other Notes About Today's Journey:** <br><br> *Suggestions:* <br><br> ✧ *Things to see and do next time* <br> ✧ *Weather conditions* <br> ✧ *Anything else you want to remember!* | |
|---|---|

# The Journey

| Departure: | Date: | | Time: | | Holiday? ❑ Yes ❑ No |
|---|---|---|---|---|---|
| **Departed From**: | | | | | |
| **Destination**: | | | | | |
| **Arrival**: | Time: | | Hours Traveled: | | |
| **Mileage**: | Start: | End: | | Total: | |
| **Planned Travel Routes**: | | | | | |

# Along the Way

| My Notes Along the Way: <br><br> *Suggestions:* <br><br> ✧ *Attractions* <br> ✧ *Cities and towns traveled through* <br> ✧ *Eats and treats* <br> ✧ *Points of interest* <br> ✧ *Routes followed* <br> ✧ *Routes to avoid* <br> ✧ *Scenic views* <br> ✧ *Shopping* <br> ✧ *Wildlife seen* <br> ✧ *Anything else you experience along the way!* | |
|---|---|

# Day's End

| Stayed Overnight: | ❑ Campground   ❑ Cracker Barrel   ❑ Walmart   ❑ Other: |
|---|---|
| **Campground Name:** | Site #:          Cost: |
| **Campground Notes:** | ❑ Full Hookups   ❑ 50-amp   ❑ Showers   ❑ Laundry   ❑ RV Dump   ❑ Wi-Fi   ❑ Camp Store<br><br><br><br><br>*Noise:* ❑ Quiet ❑ Some ❑ Noisy  •  *Overall:* ❑ Poor ❑ Fair ❑ Good ❑ Excellent |
| **Overnight Parking Notes:** | <br><br>*Noise:* ❑ Quiet ❑ Some ❑ Noisy  •  *Overall:* ❑ Poor ❑ Fair ❑ Good ❑ Excellent |
| **Dinner:** | |
| **People Met Today:** | |

# Miscellaneous Notes

| Other Notes About Today's Journey:<br><br>*Suggestions:*<br><br>✧  *Things to see and do next time*<br>✧  *Weather conditions*<br>✧  *Anything else you want to remember!* | |
|---|---|

# The Journey

| Departure: | Date: | Time: | Holiday? ☐ Yes ☐ No |
|---|---|---|---|
| **Departed From**: | | | |
| **Destination**: | | | |
| **Arrival**: | Time: | Hours Traveled: | |
| **Mileage**: | Start: | End: | Total: |
| **Planned Travel Routes**: | | | |

# Along the Way

**My Notes Along the Way**:

*Suggestions:*

- ✧ *Attractions*
- ✧ *Cities and towns traveled through*
- ✧ *Eats and treats*
- ✧ *Points of interest*
- ✧ *Routes followed*
- ✧ *Routes to avoid*
- ✧ *Scenic views*
- ✧ *Shopping*
- ✧ *Wildlife seen*
- ✧ *Anything else you experience along the way!*

# Day's End

| Stayed Overnight: | ❑ Campground   ❑ Cracker Barrel   ❑ Walmart   ❑ Other: |
|---|---|
| **Campground Name:** | Site #:          Cost: |
| **Campground Notes:** | ❑ Full Hookups   ❑ 50-amp   ❑ Showers   ❑ Laundry   ❑ RV Dump   ❑ Wi-Fi   ❑ Camp Store<br><br><br><br><br><br><br>*Noise:* ❑ Quiet ❑ Some ❑ Noisy ◆ *Overall:* ❑ Poor ❑ Fair ❑ Good ❑ Excellent |
| **Overnight Parking Notes:** | <br><br><br>*Noise:* ❑ Quiet ❑ Some ❑ Noisy ◆ *Overall:* ❑ Poor ❑ Fair ❑ Good ❑ Excellent |
| **Dinner:** | |
| **People Met Today:** | |

# Miscellaneous Notes

| Other Notes About Today's Journey:<br><br>*Suggestions:*<br><br>✧ *Things to see and do next time*<br>✧ *Weather conditions*<br>✧ *Anything else you want to remember!* | |
|---|---|

# The Journey

| Departure: | Date: | Time: | Holiday? ☐ Yes ☐ No |
|---|---|---|---|
| **Departed From:** | | | |
| **Destination:** | | | |
| **Arrival:** | Time: | Hours Traveled: | |
| **Mileage:** | Start: | End: | Total: |
| **Planned Travel Routes:** | | | |

# Along the Way

**My Notes Along the Way:**

*Suggestions:*

✧ *Attractions*
✧ *Cities and towns traveled through*
✧ *Eats and treats*
✧ *Points of interest*
✧ *Routes followed*
✧ *Routes to avoid*
✧ *Scenic views*
✧ *Shopping*
✧ *Wildlife seen*
✧ *Anything else you experience along the way!*

# Day's End

| Stayed Overnight: | ❏ Campground ❏ Cracker Barrel ❏ Walmart ❏ Other: |
|---|---|
| **Campground Name:** | Site #: Cost: |
| **Campground Notes:** | ❏ Full Hookups ❏ 50-amp ❏ Showers ❏ Laundry ❏ RV Dump ❏ Wi-Fi ❏ Camp Store<br><br><br><br><br><br>*Noise:* ❏ Quiet ❏ Some ❏ Noisy ◆ *Overall:* ❏ Poor ❏ Fair ❏ Good ❏ Excellent |
| **Overnight Parking Notes:** | <br><br><br>*Noise:* ❏ Quiet ❏ Some ❏ Noisy ◆ *Overall:* ❏ Poor ❏ Fair ❏ Good ❏ Excellent |
| **Dinner:** | |
| **People Met Today:** | |

# Miscellaneous Notes

| Other Notes About Today's Journey:<br><br>*Suggestions:*<br><br>✧ *Things to see and do next time*<br>✧ *Weather conditions*<br>✧ *Anything else you want to remember!* | |
|---|---|

# The Journey

| Departure: | Date: | Time: | Holiday? ❑ Yes ❑ No |
|---|---|---|---|
| **Departed From**: | | | |
| **Destination**: | | | |
| **Arrival**: | Time: | Hours Traveled: | |
| **Mileage**: | Start: | End: | Total: |
| **Planned Travel Routes**: | | | |

# Along the Way

**My Notes Along the Way**:

*Suggestions:*

✧ *Attractions*

✧ *Cities and towns traveled through*

✧ *Eats and treats*

✧ *Points of interest*

✧ *Routes followed*

✧ *Routes to avoid*

✧ *Scenic views*

✧ *Shopping*

✧ *Wildlife seen*

✧ *Anything else you experience along the way!*

# Day's End

| Stayed Overnight: | ❑ Campground ❑ Cracker Barrel ❑ Walmart ❑ Other: |
|---|---|
| **Campground Name:** | Site #: Cost: |
| **Campground Notes:** | ❑ Full Hookups ❑ 50-amp ❑ Showers ❑ Laundry ❑ RV Dump ❑ Wi-Fi ❑ Camp Store<br><br><br><br><br><br>*Noise:* ❑ Quiet ❑ Some ❑ Noisy ◆ *Overall:* ❑ Poor ❑ Fair ❑ Good ❑ Excellent |
| **Overnight Parking Notes:** | <br><br>*Noise:* ❑ Quiet ❑ Some ❑ Noisy ◆ *Overall:* ❑ Poor ❑ Fair ❑ Good ❑ Excellent |
| **Dinner:** | |
| **People Met Today:** | |

# Miscellaneous Notes

| Other Notes About Today's Journey:<br><br>*Suggestions:*<br><br>✧ *Things to see and do next time*<br>✧ *Weather conditions*<br>✧ *Anything else you want to remember!* | |
|---|---|

# The Journey

| Departure: | Date: | Time: | Holiday? ☐ Yes ☐ No |
|---|---|---|---|
| **Departed From:** | | | |
| **Destination:** | | | |
| **Arrival:** | Time: | Hours Traveled: | |
| **Mileage:** | Start: | End: | Total: |
| **Planned Travel Routes:** | | | |

# Along the Way

| **My Notes Along the Way:** *Suggestions:* ✧ *Attractions* ✧ *Cities and towns traveled through* ✧ *Eats and treats* ✧ *Points of interest* ✧ *Routes followed* ✧ *Routes to avoid* ✧ *Scenic views* ✧ *Shopping* ✧ *Wildlife seen* ✧ *Anything else you experience along the way!* | |
|---|---|

# Day's End

| | |
|---|---|
| **Stayed Overnight**: | ❑ Campground ❑ Cracker Barrel ❑ Walmart ❑ Other: |
| **Campground Name**: | Site #: Cost: |
| **Campground Notes**: | ❑ Full Hookups ❑ 50-amp ❑ Showers ❑ Laundry ❑ RV Dump ❑ Wi-Fi ❑ Camp Store |
| | |
| | *Noise:* ❑ Quiet ❑ Some ❑ Noisy ◆ *Overall:* ❑ Poor ❑ Fair ❑ Good ❑ Excellent |
| **Overnight Parking Notes**: | |
| | *Noise:* ❑ Quiet ❑ Some ❑ Noisy ◆ *Overall:* ❑ Poor ❑ Fair ❑ Good ❑ Excellent |
| **Dinner**: | |
| **People Met Today**: | |

# Miscellaneous Notes

| | |
|---|---|
| **Other Notes About Today's Journey**: <br><br> *Suggestions:* <br><br> ✧ *Things to see and do next time* <br> ✧ *Weather conditions* <br> ✧ *Anything else you want to remember!* | |

# The Journey

| Departure: | Date: | Time: | Holiday? ❑ Yes ❑ No |
|---|---|---|---|
| **Departed From**: | | | |
| **Destination**: | | | |
| **Arrival**: | Time: | Hours Traveled: | |
| **Mileage**: | Start: | End: | Total: |
| **Planned Travel Routes**: | | | |

# Along the Way

**My Notes Along the Way**:

*Suggestions:*

✧ *Attractions*

✧ *Cities and towns traveled through*

✧ *Eats and treats*

✧ *Points of interest*

✧ *Routes followed*

✧ *Routes to avoid*

✧ *Scenic views*

✧ *Shopping*

✧ *Wildlife seen*

✧ *Anything else you experience along the way!*

# Day's End

| Stayed Overnight: | ❏ Campground ❏ Cracker Barrel ❏ Walmart ❏ Other: |
|---|---|
| **Campground Name:** | Site #: Cost: |
| **Campground Notes:** | ❏ Full Hookups ❏ 50-amp ❏ Showers ❏ Laundry ❏ RV Dump ❏ Wi-Fi ❏ Camp Store <br><br><br><br><br> *Noise:* ❏ Quiet ❏ Some ❏ Noisy ◆ *Overall:* ❏ Poor ❏ Fair ❏ Good ❏ Excellent |
| **Overnight Parking Notes:** | <br><br> *Noise:* ❏ Quiet ❏ Some ❏ Noisy ◆ *Overall:* ❏ Poor ❏ Fair ❏ Good ❏ Excellent |
| **Dinner:** | |
| **People Met Today:** | |

# Miscellaneous Notes

| **Other Notes About Today's Journey:** <br><br> *Suggestions:* <br><br> ✧ *Things to see and do next time* <br> ✧ *Weather conditions* <br> ✧ *Anything else you want to remember!* | |
|---|---|

# The Journey

| Departure: | Date: | | Time: | Holiday? ☐ Yes ☐ No |
|---|---|---|---|---|
| **Departed From:** | | | | |
| **Destination:** | | | | |
| **Arrival:** | Time: | | Hours Traveled: | |
| **Mileage:** | Start: | End: | Total: | |
| **Planned Travel Routes:** | | | | |

# Along the Way

| **My Notes Along the Way:**<br><br>*Suggestions:*<br><br>✧  *Attractions*<br>✧  *Cities and towns traveled through*<br>✧  *Eats and treats*<br>✧  *Points of interest*<br>✧  *Routes followed*<br>✧  *Routes to avoid*<br>✧  *Scenic views*<br>✧  *Shopping*<br>✧  *Wildlife seen*<br>✧  *Anything else you experience along the way!* | |
|---|---|

# Day's End

| | |
|---|---|
| **Stayed Overnight:** | ❑ Campground    ❑ Cracker Barrel    ❑ Walmart    ❑ Other: |
| **Campground Name:** | Site #:          Cost: |
| **Campground Notes:** | ❑ Full Hookups    ❑ 50-amp    ❑ Showers    ❑ Laundry    ❑ RV Dump    ❑ Wi-Fi    ❑ Camp Store <br><br><br><br><br><br> *Noise:* ❑ Quiet  ❑ Some  ❑ Noisy  ◆  *Overall:* ❑ Poor  ❑ Fair  ❑ Good  ❑ Excellent |
| **Overnight Parking Notes:** | <br><br><br> *Noise:* ❑ Quiet  ❑ Some  ❑ Noisy  ◆  *Overall:* ❑ Poor  ❑ Fair  ❑ Good  ❑ Excellent |
| **Dinner:** | |
| **People Met Today:** | |

# Miscellaneous Notes

| | |
|---|---|
| **Other Notes About Today's Journey:** <br><br> *Suggestions:* <br><br> ✧ *Things to see and do next time* <br> ✧ *Weather conditions* <br> ✧ *Anything else you want to remember!* | |

# The Journey

| Departure: | Date: | | Time: | | Holiday? ☐ Yes ☐ No |
|---|---|---|---|---|---|
| **Departed From:** | | | | | |
| **Destination:** | | | | | |
| **Arrival:** | Time: | | Hours Traveled: | | |
| **Mileage:** | Start: | End: | | Total: | |
| **Planned Travel Routes:** | | | | | |

# Along the Way

**My Notes Along the Way:**

*Suggestions:*

- ✧ *Attractions*
- ✧ *Cities and towns traveled through*
- ✧ *Eats and treats*
- ✧ *Points of interest*
- ✧ *Routes followed*
- ✧ *Routes to avoid*
- ✧ *Scenic views*
- ✧ *Shopping*
- ✧ *Wildlife seen*
- ✧ *Anything else you experience along the way!*

# Day's End

| Stayed Overnight: | ❑ Campground    ❑ Cracker Barrel    ❑ Walmart    ❑ Other: |
|---|---|
| **Campground Name:** | Site #:          Cost: |
| **Campground Notes:** | ❑ Full Hookups    ❑ 50-amp    ❑ Showers    ❑ Laundry    ❑ RV Dump    ❑ Wi-Fi    ❑ Camp Store<br><br><br><br><br>*Noise:* ❑ Quiet ❑ Some ❑ Noisy  ◆  *Overall:* ❑ Poor ❑ Fair ❑ Good ❑ Excellent |
| **Overnight Parking Notes:** | <br><br>*Noise:* ❑ Quiet ❑ Some ❑ Noisy  ◆  *Overall:* ❑ Poor ❑ Fair ❑ Good ❑ Excellent |
| **Dinner:** | |
| **People Met Today:** | |

# Miscellaneous Notes

| **Other Notes About Today's Journey:**<br><br>*Suggestions:*<br><br>✧ *Things to see and do next time*<br>✧ *Weather conditions*<br>✧ *Anything else you want to remember!* | |
|---|---|

# The Journey

| Departure: | Date: | Time: | Holiday? ☐ Yes ☐ No |
|---|---|---|---|
| **Departed From:** | | | |
| **Destination:** | | | |
| **Arrival:** | Time: | Hours Traveled: | |
| **Mileage:** | Start: | End: | Total: |
| **Planned Travel Routes:** | | | |

# Along the Way

**My Notes Along the Way:**

*Suggestions:*

✧ *Attractions*

✧ *Cities and towns traveled through*

✧ *Eats and treats*

✧ *Points of interest*

✧ *Routes followed*

✧ *Routes to avoid*

✧ *Scenic views*

✧ *Shopping*

✧ *Wildlife seen*

✧ *Anything else you experience along the way!*

# Day's End

| Stayed Overnight: | ❑ Campground   ❑ Cracker Barrel   ❑ Walmart   ❑ Other: |
|---|---|
| **Campground Name:** | Site #:          Cost: |
| **Campground Notes:** | ❑ Full Hookups   ❑ 50-amp   ❑ Showers   ❑ Laundry   ❑ RV Dump   ❑ Wi-Fi   ❑ Camp Store<br><br><br><br><br><br>*Noise:* ❑ Quiet  ❑ Some  ❑ Noisy  •  *Overall:* ❑ Poor  ❑ Fair  ❑ Good  ❑ Excellent |
| **Overnight Parking Notes:** | <br><br>*Noise:* ❑ Quiet  ❑ Some  ❑ Noisy  •  *Overall:* ❑ Poor  ❑ Fair  ❑ Good  ❑ Excellent |
| **Dinner:** | |
| **People Met Today:** | |

# Miscellaneous Notes

| **Other Notes About Today's Journey:**<br><br>*Suggestions:*<br><br>✧  *Things to see and do next time*<br><br>✧  *Weather conditions*<br><br>✧  *Anything else you want to remember!* | |
|---|---|

# The Journey

| Departure: | Date: | | Time: | | Holiday? ☐ Yes ☐ No |
|---|---|---|---|---|---|
| **Departed From:** | | | | | |
| **Destination:** | | | | | |
| **Arrival:** | Time: | | Hours Traveled: | | |
| **Mileage:** | Start: | End: | | Total: | |
| **Planned Travel Routes:** | | | | | |

# Along the Way

| **My Notes Along the Way:** *Suggestions:* ✦ *Attractions* ✦ *Cities and towns traveled through* ✦ *Eats and treats* ✦ *Points of interest* ✦ *Routes followed* ✦ *Routes to avoid* ✦ *Scenic views* ✦ *Shopping* ✦ *Wildlife seen* ✦ *Anything else you experience along the way!* | |
|---|---|

# Day's End

| Stayed Overnight: | ❑ Campground   ❑ Cracker Barrel   ❑ Walmart   ❑ Other: |
|---|---|
| **Campground Name:** | Site #:          Cost: |
| **Campground Notes:** | ❑ Full Hookups   ❑ 50-amp   ❑ Showers   ❑ Laundry   ❑ RV Dump   ❑ Wi-Fi   ❑ Camp Store |
| | |
| | |
| | *Noise:* ❑ Quiet ❑ Some ❑ Noisy ◆ *Overall:* ❑ Poor ❑ Fair ❑ Good ❑ Excellent |
| **Overnight Parking Notes:** | |
| | *Noise:* ❑ Quiet ❑ Some ❑ Noisy ◆ *Overall:* ❑ Poor ❑ Fair ❑ Good ❑ Excellent |
| **Dinner:** | |
| **People Met Today:** | |

# Miscellaneous Notes

| **Other Notes About Today's Journey:** *Suggestions:* ✧ *Things to see and do next time* ✧ *Weather conditions* ✧ *Anything else you want to remember!* | |
|---|---|

# The Journey

| Departure: | Date: | Time: | Holiday? ☐ Yes ☐ No |
|---|---|---|---|
| **Departed From:** | | | |
| **Destination:** | | | |
| **Arrival:** | Time: | Hours Traveled: | |
| **Mileage:** | Start: | End: | Total: |
| **Planned Travel Routes:** | | | |

# Along the Way

| My Notes Along the Way:<br><br>*Suggestions:*<br><br>✧ *Attractions*<br>✧ *Cities and towns traveled through*<br>✧ *Eats and treats*<br>✧ *Points of interest*<br>✧ *Routes followed*<br>✧ *Routes to avoid*<br>✧ *Scenic views*<br>✧ *Shopping*<br>✧ *Wildlife seen*<br>✧ *Anything else you experience along the way!* | |
|---|---|

# Day's End

| Stayed Overnight: | ❑ Campground ❑ Cracker Barrel ❑ Walmart ❑ Other: |
|---|---|
| **Campground Name:** | Site #: Cost: |
| **Campground Notes:** | ❑ Full Hookups ❑ 50-amp ❑ Showers ❑ Laundry ❑ RV Dump ❑ Wi-Fi ❑ Camp Store |
| | |
| | *Noise:* ❑ Quiet ❑ Some ❑ Noisy ⬧ *Overall:* ❑ Poor ❑ Fair ❑ Good ❑ Excellent |
| **Overnight Parking Notes:** | |
| | *Noise:* ❑ Quiet ❑ Some ❑ Noisy ⬧ *Overall:* ❑ Poor ❑ Fair ❑ Good ❑ Excellent |
| **Dinner:** | |
| **People Met Today:** | |

# Miscellaneous Notes

| **Other Notes About Today's Journey:** *Suggestions:* ⬧ *Things to see and do next time* ⬧ *Weather conditions* ⬧ *Anything else you want to remember!* | |
|---|---|

# The Journey

| Departure: | Date: | Time: | Holiday? ☐ Yes ☐ No |
|---|---|---|---|
| **Departed From**: | | | |
| **Destination**: | | | |
| **Arrival**: | Time: | Hours Traveled: | |
| **Mileage**: | Start: | End: | Total: |
| **Planned Travel Routes**: | | | |

# Along the Way

| My Notes Along the Way:<br><br>*Suggestions:*<br><br>✧ *Attractions*<br>✧ *Cities and towns traveled through*<br>✧ *Eats and treats*<br>✧ *Points of interest*<br>✧ *Routes followed*<br>✧ *Routes to avoid*<br>✧ *Scenic views*<br>✧ *Shopping*<br>✧ *Wildlife seen*<br>✧ *Anything else you experience along the way!* | |
|---|---|

# Day's End

| Stayed Overnight: | ☐ Campground   ☐ Cracker Barrel   ☐ Walmart   ☐ Other: |
|---|---|
| **Campground Name:** | Site #:                Cost: |
| **Campground Notes:** | ☐ Full Hookups   ☐ 50-amp   ☐ Showers   ☐ Laundry   ☐ RV Dump   ☐ Wi-Fi   ☐ Camp Store<br><br><br><br><br><br>*Noise:* ☐ Quiet ☐ Some ☐ Noisy • *Overall:* ☐ Poor ☐ Fair ☐ Good ☐ Excellent |
| **Overnight Parking Notes:** | <br><br><br>*Noise:* ☐ Quiet ☐ Some ☐ Noisy • *Overall:* ☐ Poor ☐ Fair ☐ Good ☐ Excellent |
| **Dinner:** | |
| **People Met Today:** | |

# Miscellaneous Notes

| **Other Notes About Today's Journey:**<br><br>*Suggestions:*<br><br>✧ *Things to see and do next time*<br>✧ *Weather conditions*<br>✧ *Anything else you want to remember!* | |
|---|---|

# The Journey

| Departure: | Date: | Time: | Holiday? ☐ Yes ☐ No |
|---|---|---|---|
| **Departed From:** | | | |
| **Destination:** | | | |
| **Arrival:** | Time: | Hours Traveled: | |
| **Mileage:** | Start: | End: | Total: |
| **Planned Travel Routes:** | | | |

# Along the Way

**My Notes Along the Way:**

*Suggestions:*

✧  *Attractions*

✧  *Cities and towns traveled through*

✧  *Eats and treats*

✧  *Points of interest*

✧  *Routes followed*

✧  *Routes to avoid*

✧  *Scenic views*

✧  *Shopping*

✧  *Wildlife seen*

✧  *Anything else you experience along the way!*

# Day's End

| Stayed Overnight: | ❑ Campground ❑ Cracker Barrel ❑ Walmart ❑ Other: |
|---|---|
| Campground Name: | Site #:     Cost: |
| Campground Notes: | ❑ Full Hookups ❑ 50-amp ❑ Showers ❑ Laundry ❑ RV Dump ❑ Wi-Fi ❑ Camp Store <br><br><br><br><br><br> *Noise:* ❑ Quiet ❑ Some ❑ Noisy • *Overall:* ❑ Poor ❑ Fair ❑ Good ❑ Excellent |
| Overnight Parking Notes: | <br><br> *Noise:* ❑ Quiet ❑ Some ❑ Noisy • *Overall:* ❑ Poor ❑ Fair ❑ Good ❑ Excellent |
| Dinner: | |
| People Met Today: | |

# Miscellaneous Notes

| Other Notes About Today's Journey: <br><br> *Suggestions:* <br><br> ✧ *Things to see and do next time* <br> ✧ *Weather conditions* <br> ✧ *Anything else you want to remember!* | |
|---|---|

# The Journey

| Departure: | Date: | | Time: | | Holiday? ☐ Yes ☐ No |
|---|---|---|---|---|---|
| **Departed From:** | | | | | |
| **Destination:** | | | | | |
| **Arrival:** | Time: | | Hours Traveled: | | |
| **Mileage:** | Start: | End: | | Total: | |
| **Planned Travel Routes:** | | | | | |

# Along the Way

**My Notes Along the Way:**

*Suggestions:*

✧ *Attractions*

✧ *Cities and towns traveled through*

✧ *Eats and treats*

✧ *Points of interest*

✧ *Routes followed*

✧ *Routes to avoid*

✧ *Scenic views*

✧ *Shopping*

✧ *Wildlife seen*

✧ *Anything else you experience along the way!*

# Day's End

| Stayed Overnight: | ❑ Campground   ❑ Cracker Barrel   ❑ Walmart   ❑ Other: |
|---|---|
| **Campground Name:** | Site #:          Cost: |
| **Campground Notes:** | ❑ Full Hookups   ❑ 50-amp   ❑ Showers   ❑ Laundry   ❑ RV Dump   ❑ Wi-Fi   ❑ Camp Store<br><br><br><br><br>*Noise:* ❑ Quiet ❑ Some ❑ Noisy ◆ *Overall:* ❑ Poor ❑ Fair ❑ Good ❑ Excellent |
| **Overnight Parking Notes:** | <br><br>*Noise:* ❑ Quiet ❑ Some ❑ Noisy ◆ *Overall:* ❑ Poor ❑ Fair ❑ Good ❑ Excellent |
| **Dinner:** | |
| **People Met Today:** | |

# Miscellaneous Notes

| Other Notes About Today's Journey:<br><br>*Suggestions:*<br><br>✦ *Things to see and do next time*<br>✦ *Weather conditions*<br>✦ *Anything else you want to remember!* | |
|---|---|

# The Journey

| Departure: | Date: | | Time: | | Holiday? ☐ Yes ☐ No |
|---|---|---|---|---|---|
| **Departed From:** | | | | | |
| **Destination:** | | | | | |
| **Arrival:** | Time: | | Hours Traveled: | | |
| **Mileage:** | Start: | End: | | Total: | |
| **Planned Travel Routes:** | | | | | |

# Along the Way

**My Notes Along the Way:**

*Suggestions:*

- ✧ *Attractions*
- ✧ *Cities and towns traveled through*
- ✧ *Eats and treats*
- ✧ *Points of interest*
- ✧ *Routes followed*
- ✧ *Routes to avoid*
- ✧ *Scenic views*
- ✧ *Shopping*
- ✧ *Wildlife seen*
- ✧ *Anything else you experience along the way!*

# Day's End

| Stayed Overnight: | ❑ Campground   ❑ Cracker Barrel   ❑ Walmart   ❑ Other: |
|---|---|
| **Campground Name:** | Site #:            Cost: |
| **Campground Notes:** | ❑ Full Hookups   ❑ 50-amp   ❑ Showers   ❑ Laundry   ❑ RV Dump   ❑ Wi-Fi   ❑ Camp Store<br><br><br><br><br><br>*Noise:* ❑ Quiet  ❑ Some  ❑ Noisy  •  *Overall:* ❑ Poor  ❑ Fair  ❑ Good  ❑ Excellent |
| **Overnight Parking Notes:** | <br><br><br>*Noise:* ❑ Quiet  ❑ Some  ❑ Noisy  •  *Overall:* ❑ Poor  ❑ Fair  ❑ Good  ❑ Excellent |
| **Dinner:** | |
| **People Met Today:** | |

# Miscellaneous Notes

| Other Notes About Today's Journey:<br><br>*Suggestions:*<br><br>✧  *Things to see and do next time*<br>✧  *Weather conditions*<br>✧  *Anything else you want to remember!* | |
|---|---|

# The Journey

| Departure: | Date: | | Time: | Holiday?  ❑ Yes ❑ No |
|---|---|---|---|---|
| **Departed From:** | | | | |
| **Destination:** | | | | |
| **Arrival:** | Time: | | Hours Traveled: | |
| **Mileage:** | Start: | End: | Total: | |
| **Planned Travel Routes:** | | | | |

# Along the Way

**My Notes Along the Way:**

*Suggestions:*

- ✧ *Attractions*
- ✧ *Cities and towns traveled through*
- ✧ *Eats and treats*
- ✧ *Points of interest*
- ✧ *Routes followed*
- ✧ *Routes to avoid*
- ✧ *Scenic views*
- ✧ *Shopping*
- ✧ *Wildlife seen*
- ✧ *Anything else you experience along the way!*

# Day's End

| Stayed Overnight: | ❑ Campground    ❑ Cracker Barrel    ❑ Walmart    ❑ Other: |
|---|---|
| **Campground Name:** | Site #:                    Cost: |
| **Campground Notes:** | ❑ Full Hookups    ❑ 50-amp    ❑ Showers    ❑ Laundry    ❑ RV Dump    ❑ Wi-Fi    ❑ Camp Store |
| | *Noise:* ❑ Quiet ❑ Some ❑ Noisy  ◆ *Overall:* ❑ Poor ❑ Fair ❑ Good ❑ Excellent |
| **Overnight Parking Notes:** | |
| | *Noise:* ❑ Quiet ❑ Some ❑ Noisy  ◆ *Overall:* ❑ Poor ❑ Fair ❑ Good ❑ Excellent |
| **Dinner:** | |
| **People Met Today:** | |

# Miscellaneous Notes

| Other Notes About Today's Journey:  *Suggestions:*  ✧ *Things to see and do next time*  ✧ *Weather conditions*  ✧ *Anything else you want to remember!* | |
|---|---|

# The Journey

| Departure: | Date: | | Time: | | Holiday?  ☐ Yes  ☐ No |
|---|---|---|---|---|---|
| **Departed From:** | | | | | |
| **Destination:** | | | | | |
| **Arrival:** | Time: | | Hours Traveled: | | |
| **Mileage:** | Start: | End: | | Total: | |
| **Planned Travel Routes:** | | | | | |

# Along the Way

**My Notes Along the Way:**

*Suggestions:*

- ✧ *Attractions*
- ✧ *Cities and towns traveled through*
- ✧ *Eats and treats*
- ✧ *Points of interest*
- ✧ *Routes followed*
- ✧ *Routes to avoid*
- ✧ *Scenic views*
- ✧ *Shopping*
- ✧ *Wildlife seen*
- ✧ *Anything else you experience along the way!*

# Day's End

| Stayed Overnight: | ❑ Campground   ❑ Cracker Barrel   ❑ Walmart   ❑ Other: |
|---|---|
| **Campground Name:** | Site #:                Cost: |
| **Campground Notes:** | ❑ Full Hookups   ❑ 50-amp   ❑ Showers   ❑ Laundry   ❑ RV Dump   ❑ Wi-Fi   ❑ Camp Store <br><br><br> *Noise:* ❑ Quiet  ❑ Some  ❑ Noisy  •  *Overall:* ❑ Poor  ❑ Fair  ❑ Good  ❑ Excellent |
| **Overnight Parking Notes:** | <br><br> *Noise:* ❑ Quiet  ❑ Some  ❑ Noisy  •  *Overall:* ❑ Poor  ❑ Fair  ❑ Good  ❑ Excellent |
| **Dinner:** | |
| **People Met Today:** | |

# Miscellaneous Notes

| Other Notes About Today's Journey: | |
|---|---|
| *Suggestions:* <br><br> ✧ *Things to see and do next time* <br> ✧ *Weather conditions* <br> ✧ *Anything else you want to remember!* | |

# The Journey

| Departure: | Date: | | Time: | Holiday? ☐ Yes ☐ No |
|---|---|---|---|---|
| **Departed From:** | | | | |
| **Destination:** | | | | |
| **Arrival:** | Time: | | Hours Traveled: | |
| **Mileage:** | Start: | End: | Total: | |
| **Planned Travel Routes:** | | | | |

# Along the Way

| My Notes Along the Way: | |
|---|---|
| *Suggestions:* | |
| ◇  *Attractions* | |
| ◇  *Cities and towns traveled through* | |
| ◇  *Eats and treats* | |
| ◇  *Points of interest* | |
| ◇  *Routes followed* | |
| ◇  *Routes to avoid* | |
| ◇  *Scenic views* | |
| ◇  *Shopping* | |
| ◇  *Wildlife seen* | |
| ◇  *Anything else you experience along the way!* | |

# Day's End

| Stayed Overnight: | ❏ Campground  ❏ Cracker Barrel  ❏ Walmart  ❏ Other: |
|---|---|
| **Campground Name:** | Site #:          Cost: |
| **Campground Notes:** | ❏ Full Hookups  ❏ 50-amp  ❏ Showers  ❏ Laundry  ❏ RV Dump  ❏ Wi-Fi  ❏ Camp Store <br><br><br><br><br><br> *Noise:* ❏ Quiet ❏ Some ❏ Noisy  ♦ *Overall:* ❏ Poor ❏ Fair ❏ Good ❏ Excellent |
| **Overnight Parking Notes:** | <br><br> *Noise:* ❏ Quiet ❏ Some ❏ Noisy  ♦ *Overall:* ❏ Poor ❏ Fair ❏ Good ❏ Excellent |
| **Dinner:** | |
| **People Met Today:** | |

# Miscellaneous Notes

| **Other Notes About Today's Journey:** *Suggestions:* ✧ *Things to see and do next time* ✧ *Weather conditions* ✧ *Anything else you want to remember!* | |
|---|---|

# The Journey

| Departure: | Date: | Time: | Holiday? ☐ Yes ☐ No |
|---|---|---|---|
| **Departed From:** | | | |
| **Destination:** | | | |
| **Arrival:** | Time: | Hours Traveled: | |
| **Mileage:** | Start: | End: | Total: |
| **Planned Travel Routes:** | | | |

# Along the Way

| My Notes Along the Way: | |
|---|---|
| *Suggestions:* | |
| ✧ *Attractions* | |
| ✧ *Cities and towns traveled through* | |
| ✧ *Eats and treats* | |
| ✧ *Points of interest* | |
| ✧ *Routes followed* | |
| ✧ *Routes to avoid* | |
| ✧ *Scenic views* | |
| ✧ *Shopping* | |
| ✧ *Wildlife seen* | |
| ✧ *Anything else you experience along the way!* | |

# Day's End

| | |
|---|---|
| **Stayed Overnight:** | ❑ Campground ❑ Cracker Barrel ❑ Walmart ❑ Other: |
| **Campground Name:** | Site #: Cost: |
| **Campground Notes:** | ❑ Full Hookups ❑ 50-amp ❑ Showers ❑ Laundry ❑ RV Dump ❑ Wi-Fi ❑ Camp Store <br><br><br><br><br> *Noise:* ❑ Quiet ❑ Some ❑ Noisy ◆ *Overall:* ❑ Poor ❑ Fair ❑ Good ❑ Excellent |
| **Overnight Parking Notes:** | <br><br> *Noise:* ❑ Quiet ❑ Some ❑ Noisy ◆ *Overall:* ❑ Poor ❑ Fair ❑ Good ❑ Excellent |
| **Dinner:** | |
| **People Met Today:** | |

# Miscellaneous Notes

| | |
|---|---|
| **Other Notes About Today's Journey:** <br><br> *Suggestions:* <br><br> ✧ *Things to see and do next time* <br> ✧ *Weather conditions* <br> ✧ *Anything else you want to remember!* | |

# The Journey

| Departure: | Date: | Time: | Holiday? ☐ Yes ☐ No |
|---|---|---|---|
| **Departed From**: | | | |
| **Destination**: | | | |
| **Arrival**: | Time: | Hours Traveled: | |
| **Mileage**: | Start: | End: | Total: |
| **Planned Travel Routes**: | | | |

# Along the Way

**My Notes Along the Way**:

*Suggestions:*

- ✧ *Attractions*
- ✧ *Cities and towns traveled through*
- ✧ *Eats and treats*
- ✧ *Points of interest*
- ✧ *Routes followed*
- ✧ *Routes to avoid*
- ✧ *Scenic views*
- ✧ *Shopping*
- ✧ *Wildlife seen*
- ✧ *Anything else you experience along the way!*

# Day's End

| Stayed Overnight: | ❑ Campground   ❑ Cracker Barrel   ❑ Walmart   ❑ Other: |
|---|---|
| **Campground Name:** | Site #:          Cost: |
| **Campground Notes:** | ❑ Full Hookups   ❑ 50-amp   ❑ Showers   ❑ Laundry   ❑ RV Dump   ❑ Wi-Fi   ❑ Camp Store <br><br><br><br><br><br>*Noise:* ❑ Quiet ❑ Some ❑ Noisy  •  *Overall:* ❑ Poor ❑ Fair ❑ Good ❑ Excellent |
| **Overnight Parking Notes:** | <br><br><br>*Noise:* ❑ Quiet ❑ Some ❑ Noisy  •  *Overall:* ❑ Poor ❑ Fair ❑ Good ❑ Excellent |
| **Dinner:** | |
| **People Met Today:** | |

# Miscellaneous Notes

| **Other Notes About Today's Journey:** <br><br>*Suggestions:* <br><br>✧  *Things to see and do next time* <br>✧  *Weather conditions* <br>✧  *Anything else you want to remember!* | |
|---|---|

# The Journey

| Departure: | Date: | Time: | Holiday? ☐ Yes ☐ No |
|---|---|---|---|
| **Departed From:** | | | |
| **Destination:** | | | |
| **Arrival:** | Time: | Hours Traveled: | |
| **Mileage:** | Start: | End: | Total: |
| **Planned Travel Routes:** | | | |

# Along the Way

**My Notes Along the Way:**

*Suggestions:*

- ✧ *Attractions*
- ✧ *Cities and towns traveled through*
- ✧ *Eats and treats*
- ✧ *Points of interest*
- ✧ *Routes followed*
- ✧ *Routes to avoid*
- ✧ *Scenic views*
- ✧ *Shopping*
- ✧ *Wildlife seen*
- ✧ *Anything else you experience along the way!*

# Day's End

| Stayed Overnight: | ❑ Campground ❑ Cracker Barrel ❑ Walmart ❑ Other: |
|---|---|
| Campground Name: | Site #: Cost: |
| Campground Notes: | ❑ Full Hookups ❑ 50-amp ❑ Showers ❑ Laundry ❑ RV Dump ❑ Wi-Fi ❑ Camp Store<br><br><br><br><br><br>*Noise:* ❑ Quiet ❑ Some ❑ Noisy  • *Overall:* ❑ Poor ❑ Fair ❑ Good ❑ Excellent |
| Overnight Parking Notes: | <br><br>*Noise:* ❑ Quiet ❑ Some ❑ Noisy  • *Overall:* ❑ Poor ❑ Fair ❑ Good ❑ Excellent |
| Dinner: | |
| People Met Today: | |

# Miscellaneous Notes

| Other Notes About Today's Journey:<br><br>*Suggestions:*<br><br>✧ *Things to see and do next time*<br><br>✧ *Weather conditions*<br><br>✧ *Anything else you want to remember!* | |
|---|---|

# The Journey

| Departure: | Date: | | Time: | | Holiday? ☐ Yes ☐ No |
|---|---|---|---|---|---|
| **Departed From:** | | | | | |
| **Destination:** | | | | | |
| **Arrival:** | Time: | | Hours Traveled: | | |
| **Mileage:** | Start: | End: | | Total: | |
| **Planned Travel Routes:** | | | | | |

# Along the Way

**My Notes Along the Way:**

*Suggestions:*

- ✧ *Attractions*
- ✧ *Cities and towns traveled through*
- ✧ *Eats and treats*
- ✧ *Points of interest*
- ✧ *Routes followed*
- ✧ *Routes to avoid*
- ✧ *Scenic views*
- ✧ *Shopping*
- ✧ *Wildlife seen*
- ✧ *Anything else you experience along the way!*

# Day's End

| Stayed Overnight: | ☐ Campground   ☐ Cracker Barrel   ☐ Walmart   ☐ Other: |
|---|---|
| **Campground Name:** | Site #:        Cost: |
| **Campground Notes:** | ☐ Full Hookups   ☐ 50-amp   ☐ Showers   ☐ Laundry   ☐ RV Dump   ☐ Wi-Fi   ☐ Camp Store<br><br><br><br><br><br>*Noise:* ☐ Quiet ☐ Some ☐ Noisy  •  *Overall:* ☐ Poor ☐ Fair ☐ Good ☐ Excellent |
| **Overnight Parking Notes:** | <br><br>*Noise:* ☐ Quiet ☐ Some ☐ Noisy  •  *Overall:* ☐ Poor ☐ Fair ☐ Good ☐ Excellent |
| **Dinner:** | |
| **People Met Today:** | |

# Miscellaneous Notes

| Other Notes About Today's Journey:<br><br>*Suggestions:*<br><br>✧ *Things to see and do next time*<br>✧ *Weather conditions*<br>✧ *Anything else you want to remember!* | |
|---|---|

# The Journey

| Departure: | Date: | Time: | Holiday? ☐ Yes ☐ No |
|---|---|---|---|
| **Departed From:** | | | |
| **Destination:** | | | |
| **Arrival:** | Time: | Hours Traveled: | |
| **Mileage:** | Start: | End: | Total: |
| **Planned Travel Routes:** | | | |

# Along the Way

**My Notes Along the Way:**

*Suggestions:*

✧ *Attractions*
✧ *Cities and towns traveled through*
✧ *Eats and treats*
✧ *Points of interest*
✧ *Routes followed*
✧ *Routes to avoid*
✧ *Scenic views*
✧ *Shopping*
✧ *Wildlife seen*
✧ *Anything else you experience along the way!*

# Day's End

| | |
|---|---|
| **Stayed Overnight:** | ❑ Campground  ❑ Cracker Barrel  ❑ Walmart  ❑ Other: |
| **Campground Name:** | Site #:          Cost: |
| **Campground Notes:** | ❑ Full Hookups  ❑ 50-amp  ❑ Showers  ❑ Laundry  ❑ RV Dump  ❑ Wi-Fi  ❑ Camp Store<br><br><br><br><br><br>*Noise:* ❑ Quiet ❑ Some ❑ Noisy ◆ *Overall:* ❑ Poor ❑ Fair ❑ Good ❑ Excellent |
| **Overnight Parking Notes:** | <br><br>*Noise:* ❑ Quiet ❑ Some ❑ Noisy ◆ *Overall:* ❑ Poor ❑ Fair ❑ Good ❑ Excellent |
| **Dinner:** | |
| **People Met Today:** | |

# Miscellaneous Notes

| | |
|---|---|
| **Other Notes About Today's Journey:**<br><br>*Suggestions:*<br><br>✧  *Things to see and do next time*<br>✧  *Weather conditions*<br>✧  *Anything else you want to remember!* | |

# The Journey

| Departure: | Date: | Time: | Holiday? ☐ Yes ☐ No |
|---|---|---|---|
| **Departed From:** | | | |
| **Destination:** | | | |
| **Arrival:** | Time: | Hours Traveled: | |
| **Mileage:** | Start: | End: | Total: |
| **Planned Travel Routes:** | | | |

# Along the Way

**My Notes Along the Way:**

*Suggestions:*

✧ *Attractions*

✧ *Cities and towns traveled through*

✧ *Eats and treats*

✧ *Points of interest*

✧ *Routes followed*

✧ *Routes to avoid*

✧ *Scenic views*

✧ *Shopping*

✧ *Wildlife seen*

✧ *Anything else you experience along the way!*

# Day's End

| Stayed Overnight: | ❑ Campground   ❑ Cracker Barrel   ❑ Walmart   ❑ Other: |
|---|---|
| **Campground Name:** | Site #:          Cost: |
| **Campground Notes:** | ❑ Full Hookups   ❑ 50-amp   ❑ Showers   ❑ Laundry   ❑ RV Dump   ❑ Wi-Fi   ❑ Camp Store <br><br><br><br><br><br> *Noise:* ❑ Quiet ❑ Some ❑ Noisy ♦ *Overall:* ❑ Poor ❑ Fair ❑ Good ❑ Excellent |
| **Overnight Parking Notes:** | <br><br> *Noise:* ❑ Quiet ❑ Some ❑ Noisy ♦ *Overall:* ❑ Poor ❑ Fair ❑ Good ❑ Excellent |
| **Dinner:** | |
| **People Met Today:** | |

# Miscellaneous Notes

| **Other Notes About Today's Journey:** *Suggestions:* ✧ *Things to see and do next time* ✧ *Weather conditions* ✧ *Anything else you want to remember!* | |
|---|---|

# The Journey

| Departure: | Date: | Time: | Holiday? ☐ Yes ☐ No |
|---|---|---|---|
| **Departed From:** | | | |
| **Destination:** | | | |
| **Arrival:** | Time: | Hours Traveled: | |
| **Mileage:** | Start: | End: | Total: |
| **Planned Travel Routes:** | | | |

# Along the Way

| My Notes Along the Way:<br><br>*Suggestions:*<br><br>✧ *Attractions*<br>✧ *Cities and towns traveled through*<br>✧ *Eats and treats*<br>✧ *Points of interest*<br>✧ *Routes followed*<br>✧ *Routes to avoid*<br>✧ *Scenic views*<br>✧ *Shopping*<br>✧ *Wildlife seen*<br>✧ *Anything else you experience along the way!* | |
|---|---|

# Day's End

| Stayed Overnight: | ❑ Campground    ❑ Cracker Barrel    ❑ Walmart    ❑ Other: |
|---|---|
| **Campground Name:** | Site #:      Cost: |
| **Campground Notes:** | ❑ Full Hookups   ❑ 50-amp   ❑ Showers   ❑ Laundry   ❑ RV Dump   ❑ Wi-Fi   ❑ Camp Store <br><br><br><br><br><br> *Noise:* ❑ Quiet ❑ Some ❑ Noisy ◆ *Overall:* ❑ Poor ❑ Fair ❑ Good ❑ Excellent |
| **Overnight Parking Notes:** | <br><br> *Noise:* ❑ Quiet ❑ Some ❑ Noisy ◆ *Overall:* ❑ Poor ❑ Fair ❑ Good ❑ Excellent |
| **Dinner:** | |
| **People Met Today:** | |

# Miscellaneous Notes

| Other Notes About Today's Journey: <br><br> *Suggestions:* <br><br> ✧ *Things to see and do next time* <br> ✧ *Weather conditions* <br> ✧ *Anything else you want to remember!* | |
|---|---|

# My Campground Logbook

My Campground Logbook is a useful tool for recording detailed information about campgrounds you visit while traveling. Our logbook is the only one with maps so you can plot the location of campgrounds within each state. You create a Table of Contents as you enter data into the logbook, identifying each campground by state, name, map reference, and page number. The detailed Campground Data Entry Form allows you to record information about each location such as:

- Entrance Fees
- Elevation
- Nearby City or Town
- Managing Agency
- Season
- Number of Campsites
- Availability of Hookups
- Campsite Fees
- Site Types and Surface
- RV Length Limits
- Discounts
- Amenities and Services
- Length of Stay Limits
- Security
- Access Road Conditions
- Campground Road Conditions
- Reservation Information
- GPS Coordinates
- Distance to Groceries and Fuel
- Nearby Attractions and Restaurants

Additionally, the data entry form has space for indicating the availability of showers, laundry room, dump station, wireless Internet access and any associated fees. You can even indicate if there is a camp store available, the price paid for ice or firewood, and if groceries are sold.

You can select checkboxes to indicate which activities are available such as boating, fishing, swimming, biking, and horseback riding. You can indicate whether boat rentals are available or if only non-motorized boating is allowed. There is also a place to indicate the availability of hiking, nature, and ATV trails.

There's a section for you to record details about the specific site you stayed in such as its levelness, size, shade, and whether it is near a lake, river, or stream. You can indicate the level of noisiness during your stay and the reception quality of TV, cell, and Wi-Fi signals. And lastly, there's space for you to make notes about anything important to you.

*My Campground Logbook is available at Amazon or other online book sellers.*

Made in the USA
Lexington, KY
14 December 2019